IN THE BEGINNING

The Creation Narrative

https://www.biblenarratives.com

Copyright © 2017 by Bible Narratives LLC
P.O. Box 7206 Hampton VA 23666

All rights reserved. No part of this book may be reproduced, scanned, or distributed in any printed or electronic form without permission.

First Edition: October 2017
Printed in the United States of America
ISBN: 978-0-692-96436-1

This book uses the King James Bible for text references and quotes. If a quote is not from the King James Bible, the abbreviated translation name will follow the quote.

Abbreviated Translations:
NKJV: The New King James Version
NIV: New International Version

IN THE BEGINNING

The Creation Narrative

Craig A. Mims

Bible Narratives LLC

Hast thou not known? hast thou not heard, that the everlasting God, the LORD, the Creator of the ends of the earth, fainteth not, neither is weary? there is no searching of his understanding.

(ISAIAH 40:28)

CONTENTS

INTRODUCTION 1

GENESIS 1:1 7

DAY ONE 23
    Earth Without Form and Void 23
    The Moving of the Holy Spirit 28
    Light and Darkness 31
    Evening and Morning 35
    Time 39

DAY TWO 47
    The Firmament 47
    Three Heavens 52

DAY THREE 57
    Seas and Land 57
    Physical Life 62

DAY FOUR 67

DAY FIVE	77
DAY SIX	87
DAY SEVEN	99
Does God Need Rest?	104
Is There Another Rest?	105
Does God Still Create?	111
CONCLUSION	117
BIBLIOGRAPHY	133
INDEX OF SCRIPTURES	137
INDEX SUBJECTS	149

INTRODUCTION

The book of Genesis is the prologue for the entire Bible. It introduces us to more than just the creation of the heaven and the earth, but the prescience of God as related to life and its importance in the creation of the world. It introduces us to key theological concepts related to the existence of man and his relationship with God. The first theological concept of the Bible is the creation of the heaven and the earth. This is central to describing how the cosmos was created, who created it, and why it was created. Though many may think that mankind's existence in the universe is infinitesimal in comparison to the existence of the cosmos, the creation of the heaven and the earth, as written about in the book of Genesis, reveals that mankind is central to the creation of the universe. The creation narrative is the beginning of God's plans for mankind according to His purpose for him. The creation is a theological motif that introduces mankind into the world in which he lives and to his place in it. There are debates on whether the creation narrative is truth or just fables. It is said that Moses, the author of Genesis, used collections of writings from those who had firsthand revelations of the events, which they had passed down through the generations until Moses, who recorded them. I have no doubt that some information concerning the creation, the fall into sin, the flood, the tower of Babel, the Hebrew patriarch and others were circulating among the congregation of the Israelites in written and oral communication. Many of these motifs were based on historical events, which were a part of who they were before and while in Egypt—it was their identity. John H. Walton said in his commentary on the methodology of writing the book of Genesis, "Our belief in inspiration suggests that God's hand was behind all of these choices. We are not content to consider the book of Genesis as simply the works of human authors."[1] I agree with this statement and will also apply it to Moses's writings of the book of Genesis, even if some of his writings were edited and came from other sources. God inspired Moses to write the book of Genesis, which includes the creation narrative

---

[1] *John H. Walton, Genesis: The NIV Application Commentary (Grand Rapids, Michigan: Zondervan, 2001), 19.*

of the heaven and the earth. Whether Moses wrote and edited some of the writings in the book of Genesis is not of great importance; God ensured their veracity through His inspired chosen leader of Israel. The existence of Israel in Egypt and God's revealing to Moses at the burning bush that He was their God (Exodus 3:6-7) were each a testimony to the patriarchs of Israel. It can be safely said that whatever writings were written through divine inspiration from God and were in circulation before Moses, he validated them by accepting them as authentic. In Exodus 19:9, God ensures the Israelites of the truthfulness of Moses's writings by speaking to him in a cloud so that they may believe Moses forever. In Numbers 12:1-14, Aaron and Miriam speak against Moses, and Miriam claims that the Lord spoke to them also. The Lord hears what they say and is angry with them. The Lord says to them that He didn't speak to Moses in visions and dreams but face-to-face, plainly, not in darkness, and Moses saw His form. God asks them, "Why then were you not afraid to speak against my servant Moses?" After the Lord departs, Miriam is made leprous. Aaron pleads for her, and Moses pleads to the Lord as well. The Lord hears Moses's plea and allows her to be leprous for seven days before her healing. This signifies the relationship between God and Moses. Because of that relationship, God valued Moses more than all of Israel and even more than their Near Eastern neighbors. Though there may have been other writings of the creation that existed, Moses's writing or editing took precedent over them all. To further give the creation narrative veracity, God gave Moses the Ten Commandments and put in them that it was He who created the heaven and the earth (Exodus 31:17), which makes Moses' account of the creation and the book of Genesis true. Today we see the Jewish people who are the descendants of the Israelites Moses led out of Egypt, back in the land God promised them. They are a testimony to the truthfulness of God's purpose for mankind. Because of their perseverance in serving a true and living God, He used Israel to bring Jesus Christ—the savior of the world—the son of God—to us. Today believers cherish the writings of the Old and New Testaments as truth and are governed by them. Their very existence is a testimony to the Word of God and its veracity. As it is written:

> *"But do not fear, O My servant Jacob, And do not be dismayed, O Israel! For behold, I will save you from afar, And your offspring from the land of their*

captivity; Jacob shall return, have rest and be at ease; No one shall make him afraid. Do not fear, O Jacob My servant," says the Lord, "For I am with you; For I will make a complete end of all the nations To which I have driven you, But I will not make a complete end of you. I will rightly correct you, For I will not leave you wholly unpunished." (Jeremiah. 46:27—28 NKJV)

This book details the creation of the heaven and the earth based on the divine inspiration of Moses and his account of the creation. It follows the creation from day one to day seven based on God's revelation to Moses. It is not deeply based in a scientific sense, but rather reveals the purpose of demonstrating how God created each day by using Bible scriptures that either support or are in parallel to it. Finally, it would prove according to Bible scriptures, that mankind is not infinitesimal to the creation of the heaven and the earth, but mankind is the reason for the creation of the heaven and earth, and he is the "crown jewel of it."

And I will bring Israel again to his habitation, and he shall feed on Carmel and Bashan, and his soul shall be satisfied upon mount Ephraim and Gilead.

(JEREMIAH 50:19)

CHAPTER 1
GENESIS 1:1

"*In the beginning, God created the heaven and the earth.*" Genesis 1:1 is a summation of the creation of the universe—a prelude to the creation narrative. It reveals the completeness of the creation without a description of its design and construction. In short, its summary is that God created the heaven (Shamayim—heaven is plural) and the earth from start to finish. It gives us a glimpse of the power and knowledge of the Creator, characterizing His omnipotence, omniscience, and sovereignty. Before we can comprehend the depth of the design and construction of the heaven and the earth, we must consider its introduction by exploring the context of Genesis 1:1—to grasp its meaning and to identify the attributes of its creator. If we can better comprehend this, it will allow us to better grasp the creation narrative at its inception.

In The Beginning—The Creation Narrative

In the English Bible, Genesis 1:1 names the creator of heaven and earth as God; "God" is the vernacular to English-speaking people. To the ancient Hebrews, God in the beginning of the creation of the heaven and the earth, is called Elohim (אֱלֹהִים 'ĕlōhîm). Though God is used in the English Bible, when transferring God to Hebrew, it can be found that God and Elohim are interchangeable during the Antediluvian period—in ancient Hebrew, Elohim is identified as plural with a singular meaning, signifying that there was more than one person of Elohim in the creation. Although Elohim is plural, the persons of Elohim act as one. Today we call Elohim the Trinity because of better discernment of scriptures through Gods' progressive revelation of Himself to us. In ancient times, the concept of Elohim was distorted from its original meaning, and changed from a unified God into fragmented gods of discord that had taken on the form of spirits, humans, animals, or objects. This distortion had begun after the Fall until Noah (who didn't deviate), and continued to the time of a Semitic traveler named Abram. It was he who God reintroduced Himself to as the one God (monotheism). Some historians say the earliest concept of monotheism existed during the late Bronze Age. The Egyptian pharaoh Amenhotep IV, who changed his name to Akhenaten ("one useful to Aten"), reigned in Egypt from 1353 to1336 BCE. Amenhotep IV developed a cult that worshiped Aten, "a cosmic power that manifest itself in the form of the sun, of light, of time, of radiance and motion,"[2] His image was the Egyptian sun disk. Egypt had other gods, but Akhenaten chose to worship Aten over all the other gods of Egypt. Amenhotep IV proclaimed that only the god of the sun's disk was to be worshiped. It is said that because of this proclamation, Akhenaten was the first to introduce monotheism to the world. If it is said that Moses was the originator of monotheism, then to say Amenhotep IV was the first to introduce monotheism would probably be true. According to the Bible, it was the patriarch Abraham who first reintroduced the concept of monotheism after mankind had vacillated from it. Abraham lived approximately 740 years prior to Amenhotep IV's (Akhenaten)[3] reign. Amenhotep IV lived either one hundred years before

---

[2] *John H. Walton, Ancient Near Eastern Thought and the Old Testament: Introducing the conceptual World of the Hebrew Bible (Grand Rapids, Michigan, Baker Publishing Group, 1952), 340.*

[3] *Eugene H. Merrill, Mark E Rooker, Michael A. Grisanti, The World And The Word: An Introduction to the Old Testament (Nashville, TN, B&H Publishing Group,2011), VXI.*

or one hundred years after the Exodus. His reign was dependent on whether Exodus' early or late dates are used.[4] In any case, the children of Israel (Abraham's descendants) was known of by the Egyptians during the early date period while Amenhotep IV ruled, as well as the late date period after the Exodus had already taken place. Amenhotep IV knew of the existence of the children of Israel in Egypt at the time of his rule. It is highly probable that Amenhotep IV got the concept of monotheism from the Israelites but distorted it from its true meaning. The God of Israel was more than the sun disk god Amenhotep IV worshiped. Elohim had become more personal to the patriarch of Israel by introducing Himself to Abraham as "El"[5]—in Hebrew, the mighty one (Genesis 14:19) and He also revealed to Abraham His actual name, Jehovah (YHWH)[6]—who is Elohim, the possessor of the heaven and the earth (Genesis 15:2).

---

[4] Eugene H. Merrill, Mark E Rooker, Michael A. Grisanti, VXII
[5] *BibleWorks 9. Software for Biblical Exegesis and Research: www.bibleworks.com, (Norfolk, Virginia: BibleWorks LLC, 2010). KJV with code, Genesis 14:19.*
[6] *BibleWorks9, KJV with code, Genesis 15:2.*

And I appeared unto Abraham, unto Isaac, and unto Jacob, by the name of God Almighty, but by my name JEHOVAH was I not known to them. (Exodus. 6:3)

This passage is not saying Abraham didn't know God as Jehovah, it was presented to Moses as a question. God is telling Moses that Abraham, Isaac, and Jacob knew God as Jehovah also. In this verse and others, God presented Himself as one, indicating that the Hebrew patriarchs believed in monotheism before entering Egypt four hundred years earlier.

Most ancient Near Eastern cultures depicted their gods as independent of one another. In many cases, the gods disagreed with one another and were at times in opposition to each other. In contrast, ancient Israel believed the persons of Elohim were one and always in agreement. This belief in a one God would always remain true if they didn't vacillate in their belief. Israel's ancient Near Eastern neighbors' definition of Elohim was in sharp contrast with Israel's. They distorted Elohim from a supernatural being to a human, animal, object, or spirits. The Apostle Paul's letter to the church affirms this when he writes, *"Who changed the truth of God into a lie, and worshipped and served the creature more than the Creator, who is blessed forever. Amen"* (Romans 1:25). At times when Israel deviated from the truth, they followed the gods of their Near Eastern neighbors. God created man for His pleasure (Isaiah 43:7; Revelation 4:11) but not without a purpose. If we turn from God, in a discernible way God reintroduces Himself to us to correct that which was distorted so that we can once again know Him (2 Chronicles 7:14; Ezekiel 18:21, 22; 33:11). Because of free will, not all will return, but for those who do, it is sufficient to achieve the purpose for which mankind was created. That is, we shall be children of God (John 1:12; Romans 8:14, 18-19; 1 John 3:1—2). Since the beginning of the creation, God has safeguarded our existence, although mankind vacillates in their belief in God. The Fall, Cain and Abel, the flood, Israel in Egypt, and the exodus are just a few examples of wavering relationships with God. When this happens, God reintroduces Himself to us by revealing who He is through His attributes that we may learn of Him (Matthew 11:29) and know Him better.

God has many attributes that define His being. John S. Feinberg, general editor of the book *"No One Like Him,"* defines God's attributes as moral and non-moral but divine.[7] According to Feinberg the moral attributes of God consist of holiness, righteousness, love, grace, mercy, long suffering, goodness, loving kindness and truth. These attributes determine God's relationship with the creatures He had created and how He treats them. Feinberg furthers says, "It is so wonderful to know that our lives and destinies are in the hands of one who is not a malignant being but a good God! To be subject to an omnipotent but evil God would terrorize us moment by moment. What a blessing to know that we are in the hands of a loving, just, and compassionate deity."[8] For this we should be in awe and comforted that the Creator is not an evil but rather a good being. God's moral attributes are the reason we should humble ourselves before Him: He is sovereign and answers to no one—there is no one like Him. According to Feinberg, the non-moral but divine attributes of God are aseity, infinity, immensity, eternity, immutability, omnipotence, sovereignty, omniscience, wisdom, unity, and simplicity. These are attributes of God

---

[7] *John S. Feinberg, Ed., No One Like Him: The Doctrine of God (Wheaton, Illinois, Crossway, 2001), 277-374.*
[8] *John S. Feinberg, Ed., No One Like Him: The Doctrine of God, 339.*

(Elohim) that don't have a standard of right and wrong. It is not to say that any of these attributes conflict with God's moral attributes but rather that these attributes exist without applying a moral standard to them. God is divine; all attributes (moral and non-moral) are a part of His being and cannot be separated—they are who God is. When Elohim demonstrates His omnipotence, He is still holy. In the creation, we see that God demonstrated His non-moral attributes more, but His moral attributes affected how He created. When creating the world, Elohim demonstrated His omnipotence, which is a non-moral attribute, but He created it out of love (John 3:16). Since the persons of Elohim agree as one, then these attributes apply to all of the persons of the Elohim, called the Trinity.

The Trinity, or Godhead, capsulizes the true meaning of the ancient Hebrew name of Elohim—it goes further to identify who the persons of Elohim are. Like Elohim, the Trinity is plural and represents the persons of the Godhead—the Father, Son, and Holy Ghost—and they are one union. In the beginning of the creation, although Elohim was plural, it was an enigma as to who made up the plurality of Elohim. As the history of civilizations advanced, God became more personal, revealing more specifically the persons of Elohim. The earliest revelation of the plurality of Elohim is Genesis 1:2, when it says, "The Spirit of God moved upon the face of the waters," which indicates the Spirit is God but also exists as an independent being. Genesis 1:2 didn't say God moved upon the face of the waters, but the Spirit did. This is a more visible revelation of His being. In Genesis 1:26, Elohim says, "Let us make man," a clearer indication of the plurality of Elohim in agreement in the beginning. Although it doesn't fully reveal who "us" is, we see the plurality of Elohim more defined in their agreement to make man. At this point, we know there was God and the Holy Spirit as was revealed in Genesis 1:2. Later, Jesus (the Son of God) defined the Holy Spirit further by identifying His masculinity. This was understood by the ancient Hebrews but was revealed in a more specific way through Jesus Christ. We know that God the Spirit can act independently according to Genesis 1:2. Jesus further defines the Spirit, informing His disciples the Spirit is a He (John 14:26), and that the Spirit is equal to Him—functioning as a separate entity (John 14:16, 16:7)—and the Spirit can be indwelling (Luke 1:15, 41, 67; Acts 2:4, 9:17). Jesus stating that He was equal to the person of the Holy Spirit opens our understanding that He was also a person of Elohim in the beginning (John 15:26, 17:5). The apostle John identifies Jesus as the Word of God, and all things were made by Him (John 1:1—3). John the Baptist knew this because God revealed this to him before he met Him (John 1:33). While on Earth, Jesus identifies another person of Elohim, the third person of Elohim, calling him the Father (Luke 10:21; Mathew 11:27). The Father makes decisions (Matthew 26:39, 42; Mark 13:32; John 6:37, 44), He governs (John 5:30, 36; 14:26), He delegates responsibility (John 5:22; 14:6), and He is one with the persons of the Godhead (John 10:30; Deuteronomy 6:4; Matthew 28:19).

Although Elohim was also defined in the Old Testament, He revealed Himself to be more personal in the New Testament. As we move past the creation of heaven and earth, mankind begins to know their Creator in a personal way. Elohim is now revealed as Jehovah Elohim, or Jehovah, which is interpreted as "I am"—the Existing One (Exodus 3:13—15, 6:3).

Arise, O God, judge the earth: for thou shalt inherit all nations. (Psalm 82:8).

Although there were other idol gods in the ancient Near East, Genesis 1:1 is written to reveal the God of Abraham, Isaac, and Jacob—Jehovah, I Am. As of 2012, there were approximately 2.2 billion Christian people who worshiped the God of the creation of the heaven and the earth, who was called Elohim in the creation and who came into the world as Emmanuel—God is with us (Matthew 1:23). To affirm Elohim as the creator, through divine inspiration, God revealed to Moses that in the beginning it was Elohim who created the heaven and the earth. The name Elohim existed long before Moses. It was used by the Canaanites the descendants Canaan the son of Ham, Noah's son, a Semitic people, who passed the name Elohim from generation to generation. The Moabite women (a descendent of Lott Abrahams nephew) that brought Samuel from the grave (1 Samuel 28:13), said she saw him as gods, interpreted in Hebrew as elohim—indicating there was a distortion of the name Elohim. The origin of its use among Semitic people can go back to Noah. This is an indication that the name Elohim predated the origin of the Semitic peoples. It was distorted in time to know how to properly worship Elohim or define His attributes after Noah and his sons—the distortion is evident in Scripture. Some scholars believe that

Elohim was used by the Canaanites and suggest that the Israelites adopted the name for themselves. This is based on the interpretation of archaeological discoveries and ancient literatures. There is no evidence that their interpretation is true; it is an assumption on their part.

Although Elohim is widely used during the Antediluvian period, it was also used during the Noahic Era and afterward. The Canaanites were the descendants of Ham, Noah's son (Genesis 10:1,6). Noah's sons Shem, Ham, and Japheth and their descendants were all familiar with Elohim (Genesis 9:1). Before the flood, God presents Himself often as Elohim (Genesis 1:26, 5:1, 24, 6:5, 6:13). Moses has a firsthand account to the creation because God speaks to Moses from mouth to mouth (Numbers 12:7—8). On Mount Sinai, God reveals to Moses that His name is Elohim and that He existed in the beginning of the creation (Exodus 20:11), which indicates that the persons of Elohim existed prior to the creation.

If Genesis 1:1 was written using the Hebrew name for God, it would be written as, "In the beginning Elohim created the heaven and the earth." The perception of the creator in the opening verse of the creation narrative will be evident. Here, the prologue to the creation narrative reveals God as a plurality of persons functioning as one. Because of Elohim's plurality, it is understandable why there was a distortion in turning to other gods; they separated Elohim into individual gods and made them separate but not equal entities. They perverted Elohim's true meaning and departed from the concept of Elohim's singularity. In time, God revealed to the Israelites more specifically who the God of creation was by using godly men and women to correct the distortion. The patriarchs and their wives were just the beginning of the revelation of Elohim to the Hebrews, their Near Eastern neighbors, and then to the whole world.

What has God revealed to us in Genesis 1:1? He exists, and He is the creator of the heaven and the earth. He is transcendent, has all authority, and does as He will. He is plural but unified; He is one. He exists outside of time and space and created the cosmos from nothing. He is omnipotent, and His power is without end and is far superior than forces of the cosmos He created. He is omniscient, knowing all things in His existence, in time and space, past, present, and future. He is the designer and builder of the cosmos. He laid its foundation and completed it with His own hands. He is sovereign. Genesis 1:1 demonstrates more of His non-moral divine attributes in creating the heaven and the earth and forming them.

Genesis 1:1 only summarizes the creation of the cosmos. When Moses wrote that in the beginning God created the heaven and the earth, God was revealing to us that it wasn't the beginning of all things, just the beginning of the creation of the cosmos. The creation doesn't inform us of the creation of angels. God revealed them to us on a need-to know-basis. What is known of them is that God created them (Psalm 148:2, 5; Colossian 1:16) and they were created before the heaven and the earth (Job 38:4—7 NIV). They are spiritual but can take on human form (Hebrews 13:2, Matthew 28:2—4). They also have names (Judges 13:17—18). Their home is in heaven, but they can descend to and ascend from the earth (Genesis 18:1—3, 19; 1, 28:12). They don't marry (Matthew 22:30) and cannot reproduce. They can be very powerful (1 Chronicles 21:15; Revelation 20:1—3). They represent God (Genesis 22:11; Luke 1:18), and they protect (Exodus 14:19—20; Mathew 2:13). They have free will and can be holy or unholy (Isaiah 14:12—14; Revelation 12:7; 2 Peter 2:4). In the creation, God chose not to give details of these supernatural beings' origin. We do know that they were created before man and are higher in the Kingdom of God than man. The Bible tells us that no man can see God's face and live (Exodus 33:20), but the angels in heaven can see the face of the Father (Matthew 18:10). "In the beginning" only applies to the creation of mankind and the cosmos that sustains us. As we progress through the six days of creation, we will see how each day is designed to eventually sustain life. Genesis 1:1 doesn't address the timeframe in which the cosmos was made. When we look at our planet and see its ability to sustain life, we realize it is wonderfully made. To look at the heavens allows us to visualize our place in the cosmos—to discern the seasons and look for signs in the heavens. It reflects our Creator and His magnificent design with purpose; that purpose is to create life in a physical form after His similitude, that it may be transformed (Genesis 5:21—24; 1 Corinthians 15:51; 1 John 3:1—2).

Where wast thou when I laid the foundations of the earth? declare, if thou hast understanding.

(JOB 38:4)

CHAPTER 2

DAY ONE

"*And the earth was without form, and void; and darkness was upon the face of the deep. And the Spirit of God moved upon the face of the waters (Genesis 1:2).*"

This passage is a part of the summarization of Genesis 1:1; a component of the entire creation of the heaven and the earth. It begins to explain the details of the creation, not in scientific terms, but as related to a broad view of the creation of the heaven and the earth to sustain life forms, which Genesis 1:2 is absent of.

Earth Without Form and Void

In the Bible, "earth" is used in scriptures in different ways. To understand how it is used in Genesis 1:2, there must be a consideration of the different ways it is used. In Hebrew,

In The Beginning—The Creation Narrative

the name earth is Eretes,[9] meaning "land" or "earth," which can be understood as land or as a broader meaning, such as a planet. The word "earth" is consistently used throughout the Bible, no matter its meaning. In Genesis 1:2, "earth" is described as a physical body of water with neither inhabitants or land. This is not to say, land didn't exist; Genesis 1:2 doesn't address it. In Genesis 1:10, after God separates the waters, dry land appears, and God names it "Earth." We see the Seraphim in Isaiah 6:3 describe the earth in its entirety; it is whole and complete, full of the glory of God and is inhabited, sustaining life. Earth can also be land absent of water. In Revelation 21:1, there are two earths, the first earth that exists today, and a second earth that is to come. The first will pass away at the coming of the second earth. When the second earth comes, it will be waterless and without the sun. In the sixth chapter of Genesis, God informs Noah that the earth will be destroyed because of wickedness. Earth here represents an earth consisting of land and water. In the seventh chapter, He describes how it would be done. The fountains from the deep are to be broken up and the rain from heaven is to fall upon the earth, flooding the whole earth.

---

[9] *BibleWorks9, KJV with code, Genesis 1:1*

Although Genesis 1:2 is an enigma concerning the earth existing land, Genesis 7:12 isn't; during the flood, the land was covered with water. There is no mystery here because the narrative starts out with the earth as dry land leading up to the flood; also, it was inhabited before the flood. In Genesis 6:17 it says, *"And, behold, I, even I, do bring a flood of waters upon the earth, to destroy all flesh, wherein is the breath of life, from under heaven; and everything that is in the earth shall die."* It is seen in this verse that everything on the land and in the heavens (sky) would die but not that which was in the waters. Genesis 7:21 brings clarity to what Genesis 6:17 is saying: *"Everything on dry land died,"* meaning all flesh on dry land died but not the flesh that was in the waters. As God called the earth dry land in Genesis 1:10, the same metaphor can be used in Genesis 6:17 concerning the earth. After the creation of the second earth in Revelation 21:1, there will be no more physical waters; they are no longer needed. The final earth will be different from the earth we are familiar with today and the earth before and immediately after the flood.

Considering this, how do we interpret "earth" in Genesis 1:2, where it seems to be an enigma? Genesis 7:11—12 explains that the fountains of the great deep were broken up while the windows of heaven were open, raining for forty days. Here we see the fountains of the deep and the rain from heaven flooding the earth (referring to land). Fountain in Hebrew is *ma'yan*, meaning "spring." The springs during the flood most likely came from the earth under the waters. Genesis 2:4 describes "a mist coming from the earth to water the whole ground." This indicates the presence of water inside of the earth's land before the flood. When the earth was broken up due to some geological event, the waters were released. The waters came from fountains of the deep and the windows of heaven, and covered the highest mountain (Genesis 7:19), extending upward on the ark fifteen cubits—half the height of the ark (30 cubits). Genesis 7:19 explains that all the waters covered the high hills—the mountains. It took ten months for the waters to recede enough for the tops of the mountains to be seen (Genesis 8:5). This is an indication that the waters covered the whole earth; the rate by which it retreated was approximately four inches a day before land appeared.[10]

---

[10] John C. Whitcomb, Henry M. Morris, *The Genesis Flood: The Biblical Record and Its Scientific Implications* (Phillipsburg, New Jersey, P&R Publishing, 2011), 5.

Eventually, the waters returned to where they came from, and the earth's land above the water dried up.

It can be deduced that the land in Genesis 1:2 had already existed but is under the waters; the earth has yet to be formed and inhabited at this time. To further add to this observation, on the third day of the creation the waters were gathered together that dry land could appear. After this, God called the dry land "earth." It is most likely land wasn't created on day three but day one, since it has already been established that water can cover the land as it was by the flood. It can be assumed that when the earth was first formed on day one, the fountains of the deep had not existed. When land appeared on the third day, the fountains were created as the land appeared, and the waters were swallowed up by the land underneath the waters that dry land might appear, as it did when the water receded in Genesis 8:7, returning to where it was released (Gen. 7:11). If God had created land in Genesis 1:10, I believe there wouldn't have been a need to gather the waters together first before He created dry land. The gathering of the waters together indicates that land had already existed in Genesis 1:2 but was under the waters. It is written in Genesis 7:22 that "all that was in the dry land died," indicating there is land that isn't dry under the waters. The land didn't just appear—it already existed under the waters after it was created in the beginning. As in the flood, in Genesis 1:2, land existed but was covered by the waters. When it became visible on the third day of the creation, God specifically called it dry land, indicating land is both above the water and below it. Genesis 1:2 is the beginning of the forming of the earth for inhabitation. Land existed, but the earth was without form and the waters covered the earth; land was subordinate to the water. Genesis 1:2 describes the earth in its early state before it was formed. When it says, the earth is "without form and void," it describes a water filled earth not yet prepared for life in the flesh; it is void of it.

The Moving of the Holy Spirit

Although there isn't life in a physical form in Genesis 1:2, there is life. According to this passage, Elohim exists in the person of Holy Spirit, and He is active—hovering over the face of the waters. The author writes that "the Spirit of God moved upon the face of the waters." All life in its physical and spiritual form is the life of Elohim—because He is the giver of life (Job 10:11—12; Psalm 36:9; Acts 17:24—25; Genesis 1:29). It is not a coincidence that Genesis 1:2 focuses on the Spirit and the water, because both are sustainers of life. The water's ability to sustain life is only temporal—all flesh needs it—but the life of the Spirit is eternal. When the flesh dies, the Spirit of life in the temporal flesh returns to its sender—God. As it is written, *"Then shall the dust return to the earth as it was: and the spirit shall return unto God who gave it" (Ecclesiastes 12:7).* This passage describes what will happen to the flesh when it dies: It decays, but the Spirit of life returns to Elohim. According to Revelation 11:1—12, in the last days, God will send two witnesses to testify of Him. The world will hate them and kill them, and the Spirit of life in them will return to God as Ecclesiastes describes. In three days, the Spirit of life will return to them from the Triune, and the witnesses will come back to life again. Here we see that the Spirit of life cannot be destroyed. He is eternal, as is God. He comes from the Triune according to its will, according to God's purpose. Lazarus was dead for four days; Jesus brought him back to life and said to Martha his sister, "I am the resurrection and the life." Jesus said in John 5:26 that "the Father has life in himself," and John 7:38—39 references the Holy Spirit as rivers of living water, which signifies that the Triune is life. In Genesis 1:2, the earth is void of life in the flesh but not in the Spirit. The Spirit of the Triune, also participated in the creation of all things, creating not only inanimate but also animated forms.

The water mentioned in Genesis 1:2 is in conjunction with the Spirit. This is not to say the water is equal to the Spirit of God, it is only a type of the Spirit as it is related to the temporal flesh. All flesh that God creates needs water to sustain the life in it (Genesis 21:15—16; Numbers 21:5). Unlike the Spirit of God, which is eternal, water is temporal and is transitory—it is only required by the carnal flesh to live. When Jesus returns, believers will have bodies fashioned like the body of Jesus Christ, which can survive eternally without food or water. These transfigured bodies will receive living water from God (John 4:10—14, 7:38; Revelation 22:1). In the new heaven and earth, there will be no more temporal water. Until that time, physical water is needed to sustain life. The presence of the Spirit of Elohim and water in Genesis 1:2 lays the foundation for the creating of flesh that has life. The life of the Spirit allows the spirit of the flesh to develop. This spirit in man is different from the Spirit of life, which is of the persons of Elohim.

Without water, the flesh cannot sustain life unless God enacts some supernatural intervention to sustain life.

Light and Darkness

And God said, let there be light: and there was light. And God saw the light, that it was good: and God divided the light from the darkness (Gen. 1:3—4).

The creation of darkness and light as visible entities constitutes major components of the creation narrative. The description in Genesis 1:3—4 reveals that when the universe was created, the darkness existed before the light because the light was created in the darkness. Here Elohim demonstrated His sovereignty over the physical order of the universe, masking the essential details of its creation by using the darkness and only giving light to the exterior of it. In the darkness, the Holy Spirit hovered over the waters, seeing all things, even within the darkness of the deep. When Scripture says, "Let there be light," it is saying, "Let light exist."

I am the Lord, and there is none else, there is no God beside me: I girded thee, though thou hast not known me: That they may know from the rising of the sun, and from the west, that there is none beside me. I am the Lord, and there is none else. I form the light, and create darkness: I make peace, and create evil: I the Lord do all these things (Isaiah 45:5—7).

Darkness and light are antonyms; in Scripture, God defines them in many ways but they are most always the opposite of each other. In Genesis 1:2, they are given a temporal existence that helps express the embodiment of the creation. Isaiah 45 reveals that they have substance because God had formed and created them. Because He created them, they are not eternal, making them inferior to His being. Outside of the forces of the universe, God has no use for them, as He proclaimed in Revelation 21:23, when He revealed that His glory was sufficient to light the Holy City, Jerusalem. Although the moon and sun didn't exist in Genesis 1:2, the darkness and light did. Their origin is of God, not of the moon and sun. The darkness covers the landscape of the heaven and the earth, obscuring the perceptibility of the universe. While in the flesh, only in the presence of light can darkness be visualized. In the land of Egypt, God sent a plague of darkness that could be felt; it lasted three days. It was so extremely dark that the Egyptians were unable to leave their places, but there was light in the places of the children of Israel (Exodus 10:21—23). When Israel was fleeing from the Egyptians, God put darkness between them and Egypt for them to escape (Exodus 14:19; Joshua 24:7). This illustrates God's sovereignty over darkness, and He can use it as He wishes. So, it is with light. God formed the light in Genesis 1:2 without the use of the sun and moon. This light was capable of being brighter than the sun. Just as with the darkness, God also uses light at will. When Saul and others were on their way to Damascus to persecute the church, he saw a bright light, brighter than the sun, which blinded him. Others with him saw the light also, but it didn't have the same effect on them (Acts 22:6, 26:13). Paul spoke of its glory, which may mean the light was at its most exalted state while shining on Saul. Even in the daytime, it was very visible and was specifically directed toward Saul more so than those around him, blinding him. He doesn't call the light the glory of the Lord; he says, "the glory of that light." Glory used here in Greek is doxa, meaning opinion, judgement, view, splendor, or exalted state. Doxa is also used for describing the Lord's glory, but the author uses caution in calling the light the glory of the Lord, although it can be construed as that. Revelation 21:23 states that the Lamb of God's glory will be the light of New Jerusalem, indicating that the Lamb's glory is greater than light—there is no need for light in His kingdom. Was the light Saul seeing the glory of the Lord? When Saul saw this light shortly afterward, he hears Jesus voice. When he spoke of the light, he praised its glory rather than the Lord's glory. He did recognize that the light came from the Lord, although he didn't claim it was the Lord's glory. Like the angels in Sodom, where the men of the city wanted to know them, they defended themselves by blinding the men of Sodom. Saul had not been converted yet; he was on a mission to destroy the church, and God blinded him with light. But unlike the men of Sodom, Saul repented and humbled himself before the Lord, and he received his sight back. We can be sure concerning the narrative of Saul that Jesus blinded him with light. The light and darkness of Genesis 1:2, the light in Egypt, and the light on the road to Damascus are demonstrations of the sovereignty of God. He has full authority over light and darkness. When the darkness and light in Genesis 1:2 are created, and formed, it is the beginning of a greater purpose, to prepare for the coming of life in the flesh. As we advance into the creation narrative, light becomes essential to life in the flesh.

Evening and Morning

And God called the light Day, and the darkness he called Night. And the evening and the morning were the first day (Gen 1:5).

When God created the darkness and light, He divided them and called the light Day. The word Day is "*Yowm*" in Hebrew; Yowm can mean day, year, or time. In Genesis 1:5, day is used as an undisclosed period of light, since the sun and moon did not exist because the earth was without form. The "Day" in Genesis 1:5 is based on a period of light, not as the revolving of the earth in the presence of the sun. Here we see God creates day-light, which becomes a function of time before the creation of the moon and sun. Day-light only represents a period in time but not the completeness of time. When God says the evening and morning were the first day, it completes the cycle of time as related to a full day in the creation, not just the day-light. When God separated the darkness and light, He called the light, day and the darkness night. These two antonyms at this point were not definitive as related to the cycle of time as we know it today using the sun and moon. They only represent the dividing of darkness and light. Later in the creation darkness (night) and light (day) become more defined. There are six evenings and mornings in the creation, which Elohim calls day. These days are not based on the rising and setting of the sun or the changing between day and night. They represent a cycle of time from the beginning to the end of a creation period. On this day, we see the creation of water, light, and land underneath the water. Although time is represented when it says evening and morning, it doesn't say time was created on the first day. Many theologians believe that time was created on the first day because it states in Genesis 1:5 that God called the light day. Light and day as written in the creation are functions of time. That doesn't mean time was created because of them. It is highly probable time was created before the creation of the cosmos—even to the time of the creation of the angels. As stated in Genesis 1:3, the Holy Spirit moved across the face of the waters before the creation of light, indicating light is not a requirement for time but can be used to measure it. In Genesis 1:3, we see movement as a function of time also, which means "light" as "day" on day one is not the benchmark for time.

Isaiah saw the Lord siting on a throne. Above God, he saw seraphim crying to each other, and they were flying

(Isaiah 6:2—6). This vision connects heaven to earth, while God was sitting on a throne, and the angels were crying to each other, Holy, holy, holy, as smoke filled the temple. The angels' movement in heaven above the Lord's throne, and the movement of the door post represent time, because there is a movement from a position. This movement can cause us to conclude that the angels were subject to time.

In Ezekiel 28:11—19, God tells Ezekiel that Satan was perfect when he was created until iniquity was found in him. Unlike God, who is immutable and cannot change, Satan was subject to change, because he changed from a perfect state to an imperfect one. This required time, which is a clear indication that Satan was subject to time, as well as the angels he deceived (Revelation 12:4). When God says "evening and morning, it is symbolic to the time created that is familiar to us. When God says evening and morning in the creation, it is only a reference to time spans (increments of time) in which He created the heaven and the earth, not the angels. Because the angels were created before the creation of the heaven and earth (Job 38:7), and as in the creation of the heaven and earth, Elohim uses time to do it, and Elohim also used time to create the angels before the creation of the heaven and earth.

But, beloved, be not ignorant of this one thing, that one day is with the Lord as a thousand years, and a thousand years as one day. (2 Peter 3:8)

In Genesis 1:5 when Elohim say evening and morning it wasn't referencing a 24-hour day. We can use the description of day when interpreting the Apostle Peter's perception of a day, who was in Jesus' inner circle and was taught by Him. Peter uses day and year as metaphors to explain how God uses time. Peter isn't saying a day is a thousand years with the Lord; he is saying a day with the Lord is as if it is a thousand years, meaning God has authority over time and is not obligated to it. A day with God can be a moment or a thousand years or more. When God speaks to Moses while writing the Ten Commandments, He says in six days He created the heaven and the earth. Day is symbolic to His time (evening and morning), which Peter doesn't give the length of it.

He hath made everything beautiful in his time: also he hath set the world in their heart, so that no man can find out the work that God maketh from the beginning to the end; (Ecclesiastes 3:11).

The universe can be created in a moment or in a span of time. Civilizations come and go, and information dissipates, unable to endure the span of time; only God is eternal. Time is not eternal and was created by Elohim.

Time

On the first day of creation, time had become a major component. Elohim, within time and space, brought into existence the heaven and the earth—water, light, and land under the waters. Darkness existed also on day one, but Elohim doesn't disclose its creation on that day; He just reveals that the darkness existed. On day one, time is represented as light (day), darkness (night), evening and morning, and the moving of the Holy Spirit. Both day and night are representatives of time, and when mentioned independently of each other, time appears to be infinite. Only when they are used together (as the rising and setting of the sun) do we see time's limitation, because a time span is visual. When Elohim says, "evening and morning," time also becomes more visual, signifying a start and finish of a time-span. Although Elohim doesn't reveal how long the evening and morning span is, we see that time isn't infinite.

In The Beginning—The Creation Narrative

Ancient Israel did not view light in the terms of physics as we do today. Their simple observation of light was that when light appears, darkness moves out of the way. When Genesis 1:18 says, "God divides the light from darkness," that is how it was perceived to be—there was a separation of darkness and light. Physicists may say you cannot divide light and darkness, but God was not communicating to Moses as a physicist would concerning light but rather how ancient Israel viewed the world around them. When God calls light day, He is referring to a period of light. Day of itself represents a period of time, and light represents what is in that period of time. Some theologians believe that "day" on the first day indicates that time was created on that day. This may be subjective though Elohim does say, "let there be light" on the first day, which indicates darkness also existed on the first day, but Elohim doesn't disclose darkness creation on that day, which indicates darkness was created before day one. On the first day, it refers to two days; light as day and the evening and morning as a day. God pairs the darkness with the light but doesn't at this point show them as a cycle of time. It isn't until the creation of the moon, sun, and stars, that darkness and light are used as a complete cycle of a specific time period. Later, ancient Israel viewed light and darkness and evening and morning as one and the same—a day, although in the beginning of the creation, it doesn't appear they were. According to the creation narrative, the light as day used by ancient Israel didn't exist until day four, but during the creation Elohim used evening and morning simultaneously with light as day, indicating that evening and morning in the creation was a period of time as light and day was when the sun, moon, and stars were created. The evening and morning didn't represent light and day but rather a period of time, from beginning to end, where all things were created on that particular day. Since darkness was not created on day one but prior to it, there had to be an evening and morning for it also. The angels in heaven were witnesses to the creation of the heaven and the earth, which also means there was a time frame (evening and morning) for their creation before the creation of the heaven and the earth.

If there is a scientific argument for the creation of time on day one, then it is good to use the fundamental equation to determine time, which is, "time equal distance divided by speed." In Genesis 1:2, it states that "the spirit of God moved across the face of the waters." In our physical world,

In The Beginning—The Creation Narrative

which God created, the very act of movement requires speed and distance. In the New King James Version of the Bible, it doesn't say moved across the face of the waters but that the Spirit was hovering over it. Hovering can mean that there is no movement taking place. A computer mouse pointer can hover over an icon before clicking on the icon. The hovering of the mouse pointer seems to indicate that there is no movement, because it is stationary. However, hovering doesn't always mean there is no motion; hovering can also mean to flutter. Deuteronomy 32:11(NIV) writes of an eagle fluttering over her young; the eagle appears to be motionless except for the flapping of her wings over her young. Although the mouse appears to be motionless, there is motion because of its hertz cycle. In comparison to the King James Version, where motion was taking place, it can be concluded that the reference to the Spirit "moved upon the face of the waters" is to mean fluttering (hovering) over the face of the waters.

Genesis 1:5 defines a difference between day and night. Elohim calls the light day and the darkness night. This is a change from Genesis 1:2, where it says, "And darkness was upon the face of the deep." After this proclamation,

Day One

Elohim said, "Let there be light," which appears that light, not darkness, was created on day one. The creation of time is dependent on when the darkness or the angels were created. According Job 38:4, 7, the angels witnessed the creation of the heaven and the earth. This means time wasn't created on day one but before. When there was a completion of a creation period, Elohim said "evening and morning." It doesn't mention the creation of angels after the creation of the heaven and the earth. We know they were created (Colossian 1:16—17; Psalm 148:2,5). In the book of Job, it reveals that the angels shouted for joy when the heavens and the earth were created, indicating time had already been created.

Time is the product of creation. If not for time, mankind and the historical events of the Bible would not exist as we know them. Time has been created to record the events of the changes in that which was created from its conception to its end. Throughout history, God reveals to mankind the coming of the end of time. The angel of God speaks to Daniel to inform him of the historic events that will happen to the Jews before the end of time (Daniel 10:14). He explains to Daniel why it took so long to reach him for deliverance. Demonic forces and their demonic ruler (the prince of Persia) had opposed the angel of God (Daniel 10:13). We know that the demonic forces over Persia were defeated because of another historical event in time that was on the horizon—the coming of Greece, and the demonic forces that influenced the people of Greece (Daniel 10:20). Historical events in time will continue to advance until the end of time as we know it. At the end of time, all historical events that unfolded in time will culminate, and for the world, it will end (Revelation 10:6). Afterward, time has no effect on the angels or the children of God. Although time has influence over the creation, God is not influenced by it nor is He subject to it. God is transcendent, and His dwelling place is outside of time and space, He can enter and leave them at will. God created time and space; they were nonexistent before the creation of all things.

In Genesis 1:5, God combines the evening and morning as day to make them a complete function for a period of time. God doesn't tell us how long it took to get from the evening to the morning, but we do know a distance existed between them, because of creation taking place on each day. When Elohim says evening and morning, it represents the completeness of a time period. If we recognize how the ancient Hebrews viewed a day, the evening represents the beginning and the morning represents the end of the day.

John H. Walton writes in his book, *"Ancient Near Eastern Thoughts and the Old Testament,"*[11] that time was created on day one. This is subjective and will appeal to those who do not believe in the veracity of the sixty-six books of the Bible. The book of Job says the angels rejoiced at the creation of the heaven and the earth, indicating time existed when the angles were created. If the darkness was created before the light, time existed when the darkness was created. Although time existed on day one, day one is not the origin of time.

---

[11] *John H Walton, Ancient Near Eastern Thought and the Old Testament: Introducing the Conceptual World of the Hebrew Bible (Grand Rapids, MI, Baker Publishing Group, 2006), 180.*

I beheld the earth, and, lo, *it was* without form, and void; and the heavens, and they *had* no light.

(JEREMIAH 4:23)

CHAPTER 3

DAY TWO

The Firmament

On the first day God created the waters, land, and light. Although the earth had not yet been formed, its foundation had been laid. In Genesis 1:6—8, the second day, God speaks to the waters creating a firmament between them. Like the first day, the second day accomplishes the same objective—the preparing of the earth for life in the flesh. In Hebrew, the word "firmament" means an extended surface (solid), expanse or sky—as describing the space between the two waters. In Genesis 1:6—8, the firmament as described by Moses was a space that was created to separate the waters. Elohim called the space heaven; "shameh (singular)"[12] which can also be interpreted as sky. The firmament that divided the waters created an atmosphere for future inhabita-

---

[12] Bible Works9, KJV with code. Genesis 1:8.

tion of the earth. Elohim using heaven as a name for firmament describes heaven as less of a solid extended surface, and more as an atmosphere between the firmament called "sky." In Genesis 7:19, after the waters covered the tops of the mountains, God stopped the waters from extending into heaven, giving truth to its existence. There should be caution in interpreting heaven as a solid because there is an absence of visible extraterrestrial bodies. Here God doesn't speak of a extraterrestrial heaven because it hadn't been revealed on day two.

In the Bible, heaven can be described as existing terrestrial, or extraterrestrial. In Genesis 1:6—8, Elohim describes heaven as terrestrial existing within the sphere of the earth. Here, Elohim specifically created heaven as an atmosphere to sustain life in the flesh. He doesn't explain how it was done in scientific terms but only allows the visualization of how heaven was created by outlining its function within the creation narrative. It can be determined that not only was the heaven a space between the two waters but the elements within it were intricate parts of an ecosystem necessary to sustain life forms. In Matthew 16:2, Jesus, talking to the Pharisees and Sadducees, described the sky as a discernable part of the earth's ecosystem. He points out the characteristics of the sky by explaining the colors of the morning and evening skies and how they can be used to discern the weather. The sky Jesus was describing was physical and can be observed. Jesus was describing a sky that was after the great flood, this sky was different from the sky in Genesis 1:7—8. The sky in Matthew 16:2—3, is similar but is more discernable than the atmosphere in Genesis 1:6—8 Elohim created on the second day. On day two rain was not common as it was in Matthew 16:2—3.

The Apostle John informs believers that Jesus was the Word of God who created all things and explains that Jesus was there in the beginning of the creation, which includes when the sky (atmosphere) was created between the waters (John 1:1-3, 14, 17, 36). The metaphor Jesus used in Matthew 16:2 was that the Pharisees and Sadducees could discern the weather but were unable to discern the coming of the Kingdom of God through the Holy Spirit, indicating that the sky had characteristics that can be observed. In Genesis 2:5—6, it indicates that rain wasn't common before the flood; the earth was watered from a mist that came up from the ground. The sky had less characteristics to discern in the creation. Rain became common in the earth in Genesis 7:4 after mankind had become corrupt to the point that God caused it to rain on the earth. Noah preached for over 100 years that it would rain, and mankind was unable to comprehend rain because it was uncommon, so they couldn't understand what Noah was saying. After approximately 120 years, it rained, and the flood covered the earth. Through Noah and his family righteousness returned to the earth because it was cleansed from unrighteousness. There was also a change in the atmosphere, and it became like the atmosphere Jesus spoke of. The rainbow became evidence of the change in the atmosphere. In Mathew 16:2—3, Jesus used the weather as metaphors to the coming of the Kingdom of God as prophesied (Daniel 2:35; Matthew 24:37—39; Luke 17:26—27). The word "heaven" is not always exclusive to the heaven in the terrestrial sphere of the earth, when addressing a single entity of heaven, it can be included as an extraterrestrial one also.

And I will make thy seed to multiply as the stars of heaven, and will give unto thy seed all these countries; and in thy seed, shall all the nations of the earth be blessed; (Gen. 26:4).

In this passage, God directs Abraham to the heaven outside of the earth's sphere and explains to him that He will bless his seed as the stars in it. This passage references the extraterrestrial bodies of stars as heaven. Though singular, it is not a reference to the heaven within the sphere of the earth. Some passages separate the terrestrial and extraterrestrial heavens by describing them as heaven and heaven of heavens. In 1 Kings 8:27, Solomon recognized the difference between the terrestrial heaven in the earth and in the extraterrestrial heaven among the stars:

But will God indeed dwell on the earth? behold, the heaven and heaven of heavens cannot contain thee; how much less this house that I have builded? (1 Kings 8:27).

Solomon recognized that God's existence exceeds the earth's heaven and extraterrestrial heaven. He asks, how can the temple be built to contain God? The answer is it cannot, because Gods omnipresence is eternal, and He exists everywhere. In this passage, Solomon is not talking about the heaven where God dwells, but only that which is within the substance of His creation. Though God's presence exists within His creation, there isn't enough space in the earthly heaven or in the extraterrestrial heaven of heavens to contain His being. In 1 King 8:30, Solomon gives recognition to another heaven, which is called the dwelling place of God. When he says heaven in this passage, he refers to it as singular also, but it is independent of the terrestrial heaven within the sphere of the earth and the extraterrestrial heaven among the stars.

Three Heavens

There are three heavens in the Bible. Two are carnal and the other spiritual. The carnal ones are represented as "heaven" and "heaven of heavens"; they are uninterrupted spaces located within the sphere of the earth and the cosmos that exists outside of the earth's sphere. The third heaven is spiritual; it is supreme and transcends the cosmos itself. All heavens act as barriers to life in the flesh. When speaking of the earth, the elements of the first heaven envelops the earth as a covering. If life in the flesh surpasses the earthly heaven, it cannot function on its own without assistance. When the fowls of the air were created, they flew within the terrestrial heaven of the earth and could not exceed above the density of its outer perimeter. The heaven within earth cannot function within the extraterrestrial heaven of the cosmos, because it was only designed for terrestrial bodies—it needs a planet to sustain it. Not all planets are designed to sustain life in the flesh, because of a deficiency of an atmosphere or ecosystem within them.

> *There are also celestial bodies, and bodies terrestrial: but the glory of the celestial is one, and the glory of the terrestrial is another. There is one glory of the sun, and another glory of the moon, and another glory of the stars: for one star differeth from another star in glory. (1Cor 15:40—41).*

In this passage, the Apostle Paul explains the mystery of the heavens. One is terrestrial and the other is celestial. When he describes the glory of sun, moon, and stars, he is referencing the second heaven or heaven of heavens —the universe that exists outside of the terrestrial body of the earth. The extraterrestrial heaven is so vast that it can't be bridged in physical form or within time and space. It is estimated that there are over one billion trillion stars in the visible universe, and it is estimated to take 13.3 billion light years to reach the furthest known galaxy; one light year is approximately six trillion miles. It is sobering to the similitude of God to only see just a glimpse of the shadow of the omnipotence, omniscience and omnipresence of the being of God.

> *Now this I say, brethren, that flesh and blood cannot inherit the kingdom of God; neither doth corruption inherit incorruption. (1Cor 15:50)*

The third heaven is where the throne of God is, and only by the grace of God can we enter there, by passing from life to death in the Lord. Paul makes a sharp contrast between flesh and blood and the Kingdom of God or Kingdom of Heaven. He explains that it is impossible for flesh and blood to possess the Kingdom of God. He further uses a metaphor to compare flesh and blood and the Kingdom of God to corruption and incorruption. This is a powerful statement that demonstrates the impossibility of flesh and blood transcending space and time to enter heaven, where God dwells, or His earthly kingdom, without the spirit of God. The first and second heaven (heaven and heaven of heavens) are physical. Only the first heaven mentioned in Genesis 1:6—8 is designed to sustain life in the flesh. As it is written in 1Corinthians 15:50, flesh and blood (life in the flesh) have no place in the third heaven, only spiritual life exists there. Jesus was informing the Pharisees and Sadducees in Matthew 16:2 that the Kingdom of God was coming and was more than the discernment of the weather but the discernment of the Holy Spirit and His righteousness, which is needed to enter the Kingdom of God where flesh and blood cannot enter. Spiritually, the Kingdom of God and Kingdom of Heaven are synonymous. It is not carnal and we are ushered into it by the Holy Spirit. Those who seek to obtain it in the flesh will not see it or enter it; only through Jesus Christ and the Holy Spirit can one enter the Kingdom of Heaven on earth. Paul recognizes that the only means of entering the third heaven is to be absent from the body. Genesis 1:6—8 does not refer to the second or third heaven called heaven of heavens and the dwelling place of God. It only refers to the heaven within the sphere of the earth between the waters. The earths heaven is a key element for the sustaining of life in the flesh due to its atmosphere that was created on the second day.

Before the advancement into the third day, we can look at the passages described as evening and morning on day one and two, how Elohim identifies each as a day by referencing time as morning and evening. On day two the time period of evening and morning allowed for the creation of the earth's heaven—heaven, was the only thing created on day two. It doesn't tell us how long it took to create the earth's heaven, but we know that it was created in a particular time period because it says evening and morning was the second day. Other than this it becomes a mystery to the increments of the time of it. It is God's time, and He is saying, "I Am," the Creator of the heavens. Whether Elohim created the earths heaven in one day or in a billion years, He is Elohim and is the great "I Am," meaning "I Exist" time is not a bearer to Me.

CHAPTER 4

DAY THREE

Seas and Land

Before day three, the earth was void of life in the flesh as we know it, although microorganisms may have existed prior to day three; as disclosed in Genesis 1:2, the Holy Spirit, a person of Elohim, the giver of life, was hovering over the face of the waters. On this day, the earth's waters were warm enough for the creation of life, but Genesis 1:2 tells us the earth was void of it. Day two, an atmosphere was created and the elements to sustain life in a physical form existed—water—land—and atmosphere. At this point, the earth had been formed to a degree to sustain physical life. Macrobian life forms on day two was not what Elohim focused on when the creation is explained to Moses. Elohim communicates to Moses the creation of more complex life-forms that can be better visualized and more easily understood as related to the existence of man. On the third day,

Elohim further divided the waters below the firmaments into seas that these more complex life-forms could be created. On this day, God gathered the waters together under the heaven (skies) into one place so that dry land may appear. This signifies that there was a major shift in water and land mass below the heavens, causing dry land to appear.

In Geneses 1:9—10, it may appear that land is created on the third day because it says, "Let the dry land appear," and Elohim calls the dry land earth. Elohim created the land when He created the heaven and the earth., but the day the land was created wasn't day three. On day one, there is no mentioning of earth as dry land. It can be argued that land didn't exist on the first day, that is, if earth on the third day is used as a reference to earth on the first day. On the third day (Genesis 1:9—10), there is dry land, and there is no mentioning of it on the first day; only water existed (Genesis 1:2). On the first day, it says the earth was void, which can be understood that only water existed. With a void earth on the first day, it can be argued that land was non-existent. When comparing the two passages, we can see that the earth on day one is not the same as the earth on day three, because day three references earth as dry land,

and on day one doesn't. Day one, doesn't say that land didn't exist; it just doesn't recognize its existence as dry land. On day one it says the earth was without form. It is not saying there was no land, but it wasn't visible as it was on day three. To say the earth was void (empty), doesn't mean it was void of land but void of life. This is the only thing that would make sense because the purpose of creating the heavens and the earth is to sustain life-forms in the flesh—all life in the flesh. A void earth on day one indicates that life in the flesh didn't exist on day one. On day two, we see an atmosphere was created, which means there was a gravitational pull on the earth; the earth had a core prior to the appearance of land on day three.

As explained in chapter two of this book, during the time of Noah, the surface of the earth was flooded. The flood was so great that it covered the tops of the mountains fifteen cubits of the draft (the waterline of a ship above its hull) of the ark. According to the Bible, the ark was thirty cubits high (Genesis 6:15). This mean fifteen cubits of the ark was below water (the draft). The draft determines the minimum depth of water a ship can safely pass through over land. This means the water had to be high enough over the mountains so that the ark could pass over. The Bible also tells us that during the flood, God opened the windows of heaven and poured out the rain on the earth so that the earth could be covered with water. The rain that was poured out upon the earth was greater than the waters above the firmament—it was a supernatural event. The place where the rain came from was more than the waters above the firmaments. God gave Israel manna in the wilderness (Exodus 16:4, Psalms 78:24), it didn't come from the dwelling place of God (John 6:31), but from heaven "Quianos"—the firmament (sky). As manna, the rain from the windows of heaven (Quianos) was a supernatural pouring out of rain from heaven that assisted the rain from the firmaments and the waters of the deep to cover the earth during the flood. The earth was covered with water on day one as was the day of the flood; The supernatural pouring out of rain from heaven was necessary to flood the earth because the geography of the earth was different in Noah's time then day one. It appears that more water was needed to cover the earth because the mountains extended into the heaven above the waters in Noah's time; on day one there were no mountains above the waters, the land was a mass and most likely denser under the waters before it was formed. Days one through three complement each other in supporting that the earth was covered with water in the beginning. Though day three was the first day when it mentioned dry land, the seas had to be gathered together for it to appear.

The term dry land, when separated from the water, is also used in Exodus 14:21—22, 29. As the children of Israel fled the Egyptians, God divided the Red Sea so they could walk across to the other side on dry land. In Joshua 4:18, 22, the Israelites' priests, the ark of the covenant, stood in the Jordan River, the water parted and the land became dry. After dry land appeared, the children of Israel walked across to the other side. The crossing of the Red Sea and Jordan River obviously were supernatural events, as was the gathering of seas so that dry land may appear on day three. Land existed, but it was under the water; when separated from the water, it is called dry land. Up to this point, we see Elohim demonstrating to us His omnipotence and omniscience in forming the earth that life may appear that the earth may be inhabited. On day three, water, land, atmosphere, and light existed. The presence of these substances prepared the way for the creation of physical life-forms on this day.

Physical Life

As we look at day three of the creation narrative, physical life in the form of vegetation was created on land. Scripture doesn't reveal to us whether vegetation existed in the seas: it only reveals its creation on land. On day three, the earth was formed to the point where physical life could sustain itself on land. It can be assumed that there was plant life in the seas since the creation of life in the flesh is first revealed coming out of the waters on day five. Microbes or single-cell organisms, although they may have existed, are not the focus of the creation on day three. The message is clear: Complex living organisms (grass, herbs, and fruit trees) are created on day three, and their creation is essential to sustaining life on Earth.

There were three forms of vegetation God created on day three: grass, herbs-yielding seed, and trees yielding-fruit. This may seem out of order in the creation narrative because the sun's creation isn't evident yet, and these plants needed light to grow and reproduce. Although God set in motion physical laws for the heaven and the earth to function, vegetation existing before the creation of the sun seemed to be an enigma. It isn't; it is a demonstration of Elohim's sovereignty. Chapter two of this book explains the creation of light on the first day; it is the same light that exists on day three when vegetation was created. In no way am I trying to explain the creation of vegetation as scientifically definitive; its creation is supernatural, as revealed in Scripture—Elohim created it. There are times in Scripture where God demonstrated His sovereignty over the physical laws He created. When God blinded Saul on the way to Damascus, only he was blinded by the light, but those who were with him weren't. This demonstration of God's sovereignty with Saul can be argued for the characteristics of the light created on day one—it can be application specific. Geneses 1:3 reveals that Elohim is the creator of light and demonstrates its use by creating vegetation and all the substances needed to sustain it. On day three, light exists, and vegetation grew and produced seeds of their own kind. It just doesn't use the sun to start the process; the light of the creation is sufficient.

If Elohim created vegetation on dry land, it is highly probable that He created vegetation in the seas in all forms, noncomplex and complex. The creation focused on the purpose of the creation narrative rather than the science of it; vegetation was created for food. As with other days, the creation narrative on day three also meets the same criteria:

purpose. The light, water, land, atmosphere, and vegetation all had the same purpose: to sustain life.

> *And I will send grass in thy fields for thy cattle, that thou mayest eat and be full. (Deut. 11:15)*

In the creation narrative, the days are created to communicate to mankind the basics and purpose of the creation. Today we understand that vegetation converts carbon dioxide back to oxygen and that vegetation growth can determine soil health. In Deuteronomy 11:15, God introduces grass as food as He gives Israel grass for their cattle to eat that they may eat and be filled. God doesn't reveal to them the other functions of grass; He reveals grass as more tangible to the existence of sustaining life. This also includes herbs and trees that bear fruit. And God said,

> *"See, I have given you every herb that yields seed which is on the face of all the earth, and every tree whose fruit yields seed; to you it shall be for food. "Also, to every beast of the earth, to every bird of the air, and to everything that creeps on the earth, in which there is life, I have given every green herb for food;" and it was so. (Gen 1:29-30 NKJV)*

As we can see, God reveals to humans the purpose of the creation of vegetation: It is to be used as food for them and for every beast of the earth, birds, and creeping things. When God speaks to Moses on Mount Sinai, He reveals to him the creation of vegetation on day three. He doesn't speak to Moses of the existence of water and land plants such as algae, fungi and other plant life that grew in the water and on land, although they may have existed. Neither did God reveal to Moses soil microbes, nor how plants produce their own food. They were not important at that time in communicating the creation of the heaven and the earth to us.

The creation of life in its vegetative form without the use of the sun demonstrates Elohim's sovereignty over His creation. He introduces light on day one that is greater than the brightness of the sun. Elohim could have created plant life without the presence of light, but He chose to stay within the physical laws of the universe He created for our understanding.

These are the generations of the heavens and of the earth when they were created, in the day that the Lord God made the earth and the heavens,

And every plant of the field before it was in the earth, and every herb of the field before it grew: for the Lord God had not caused it to rain upon the earth, and there was not a man to till the ground. (Gen 2:4-5).

This passage supports the account of the creation of vegetation written in Genesis 1:11—12. Some may say this represents a second account of the creation, giving credence to the belief that Moses used documents that were already written to formulate the Genesis account. I do not dispute the premise that Moses used the account passed downed through the patriarchs of the Israelites to write the creation. If there were any distortion concerning their accounts, Moses, the inspired leader of God, through revelation from God, set in order the truthfulness of the creation accounts to ensure its veracity; God knew Moses face to face (Deuteronomy 34:10; Numbers 12:8). When Moses writes concerning the creation of vegetation in Genesis 2:4—6, he is summarizing the creation of plant life and explains how they get their nutrition to reproduce.

CHAPTER 5

DAY FOUR

On day four a transition took place. From the beginning of the creation to the introduction of day four, we see the light created on day one active in the creation. On day four, Elohim revealed the creation of the sun, moon, and stars; to perform the functions of creating light and for the discernment of signs, seasons, days, and years. The light of the celestial bodies began to take precedence over the light that was created on day one. On day four, we see the transition of light from the light created on day one to a more distinct light that emanated from the celestial bodies; these lights are the cause of the transition. It is not to say the light from the celestial bodies was greater than the light created on the first day; it is to say Elohim created the celestial lights to perform specific purposes on day four and afterward. The creation was not done without thought. God is omniscient, and has the knowledge of all things. He creates with purpose, and God will always have a foreknowledge of the purpose of that which He creates. He is the beginning and the end (alpha and omega) of His creation. The light that was created on day one had completed its purpose as a major element in the creation of plant life preceding day four. On the fourth day, the celestial bodies—the moon, sun, and stars—were not just for illumination. They were created for signs, seasons, days, and years, and, later, as memorials to events within them. In Genesis 1:14, celestial bodies determine the periods when vegetation yields it seeds. In some cases, the yielding of their seeds can be off by a month, because of the alignment of the celestial bodies. These periods (seasons, days, and years) were later used as signs for harvest and celebration.

> *Seven weeks shalt thou number unto thee: begin to number the seven weeks from such time as thou beginnest to put the sickle to the corn. And thou shalt keep the feast of weeks unto the Lord thy God with a tribute of a freewill offering of thine hand, which thou shalt give unto the Lord thy God, according as the LORD thy God hath blessed thee: And thou shalt rejoice before the Lord thy God, thou, and thy son, and thy daughter, and thy manservant, and thy maid-*

servant, and the Levite that is within thy gates, and the stranger, and the fatherless, and the widow, that are among you, in the place which the Lord thy God hath chosen to place his name there. (Deut. 16:9—11)

In this passage, God, the creator of the heaven and the earth, commands Israel to keep the Feast of Weeks. During the Feast of Weeks, God commanded all within the borders of Israel to rejoice. The Feast of Weeks lasts for six days and occurs between May and June. It is a seasonal festival celebrating the wheat harvest and commemorating the presenting of the Ten Commandment to Israel 49 days after Israel was freed from slavery. It begins on the 50th day after Passover. In the New Testament, the Festival of Weeks is called Pentecost. It was named such by the Hellenistic Jews because it occurs 50 days after Passover. Pentecost among Christian believers has a greater significance than the harvest of wheat. It represents the beginning of the church, where there is a harvesting of souls. In Act 2:1—5, the Bible explains that when the day of Pentecost fully came, they were all filled with the Holy Ghost. In the book of Act the pouring out of the Holy Spirit to believers is called the Day of Pentecost, and it happened during the Feast of Weeks. On the day of Pentecost, the Holy Spirit became indwelling for those who were waiting on the promise. It happened in one day—although its dispensation had a more far-reaching effect than that day. The Passover occurs earlier in the spring, between March and April and lasts for one day. It celebrates the deliverance of Israel from Egypt's bondage. It coincides with the feast of Unleavened Bread, which lasts seven days and is at the same time as the barley season. The celestial bodies that were created in the book of Genesis are used by people created by God to discern the periods in which seed-bearing vegetation reproduces. Using the celestial bodies, humans can determine the time for planting and harvesting, ceremonial events, and memorials to God. They can divide these periods into hours, days, months, and years. Animals can discern the changing of seasons, which determines the time for gathering, migration, and hibernation. How living things collect food is dependent on seasons, which are influenced by the moon, sun and stars. The creation of signs, seasons, days and years is essential to the survival of moving creatures—fowl, fish, animals and humans. After the creation was complete, God used the moon, sun, and stars to coincide with events to commemorate His intersession on behalf of His people.

> "And Moses said unto the people, remember this day, in which ye came out from Egypt, out of the house of

bondage; for by strength of hand the Lord brought you out from this place: there shall no leavened bread be eaten. This day came ye out in the month Abib." (Exo 13:3-4)

This passage of Exodus, commemorates Israel being delivered from bondage in Egypt. God commands Moses to remember the month of Abib, when He brought them out. Their deliverance is called Passover, which lasted for one day.[13] God spared their first-born because of their obedience to Him, when they painted the blood of an unblemished lamb on the side posts and upper door post where they dwelled. When the destroyer saw the blood, he would pass over that place of dwelling, sparing the first born. Abib, means "young barley ears"[14]; the month of Abib is in the barley season. God commemorated the Passover and the Feast of Unleavened Bread as a memorial during this season. The Feast of the Unleavened Bread starts in the spring after the Passover and lasts seven days.[15] Following the

---

[13] *Eugene H. Merrill, Mark E. Rooker and Michael A. Grisanti, The World and Word: An Introduction to the Old Testament (Nashville, Tennessee: B&H Publishing Group, 2011), 229*
[14] *BibleWorks9, NKJ with code, Exodus 13:1-4.*
[15] *Merrill, The World and Word, 229.*

Passover, Israel was required to eat unleavened bread for seven days. Here God used the seasons, days, and years as a memorial to Him for delivering Israel from bondage. The season took on a spiritual meaning, and the barley harvest season became a sign to celebrate the Passover and Feast of Unleavened Bread. Though these memorial celebrations didn't exist on the creation of day four but rather after the completion of the heaven and the earth and the creation of man, God would use the seasons as a memorial to Him. The creation of the moon, sun, and stars for signs, seasons, days, and years went beyond the reproduction cycle of herb-yielding seed and tree-yielding fruit. During the cycle of the celestial bodies, Israel was to honor God by recognizing the memorial days, such as Passover, the Feast of Unleavened Bread, and Pentecost. These memorial celebrations within the seasons, days, and years were holy. When God said that He created the celestial bodies for signs, the signs also meant that the celestial bodies would exhibit supernatural events that would coincide with what God was doing on the earth. God used an eastern star to announce that His son was in the world (Matthew 2:2). In the second coming of Christ, God will use signs in the heavens to let the world know of His coming (Luke 21:25—26). The creation of the moon, sun, and stars for signs of seasons, days, and years on the fourth day signified that heaven and the earth were in motion; time had become more notable. The sun light during the day shone upon the earth. At night, the moon and the stars illuminated the earth, as the seasons came and went. In Genesis 1:16, it says Elohim made two great lights in the heavens. This passage differs from Genesis 1:14, which explains the creation of light without a distinction of what the lights are. Genesis 1:16 gives more detail of what the lights are as Elohim reveals their existence according to the purpose in which they were designed. He made two great lights: the moon and the sun. The sun, the greater light, rules by the day; the moon, the lesser light, rules by night. As the moon gets its illumination from the sun, at times its brightness can be seen in the day sky, appearing to act independently of the sun. When Elohim created the celestial bodies, He put the universe in motion; the seasons are evidence of that. At times, a universe in motion allows for the moon and sun to be in the sky at the same time. In Genesis 1:16, Elohim mentions the stars but gives less of an emphasis on their purpose. On the fourth day, we see that Elohim does not explain how the sun warmed the earth because the earth is already warm enough to create life. In the beginning of the creation on day one, the earth is a watery planet. But we can conclude that there was activity going on in the earth to keep it warm, laying the foundation for the existence of life-forms. Elohim revealed to Moses (Genesis 1:2) that in the beginning the earth was a watery planet that would eventually be inhabited by living things. There is no mentioning that the earth was an icy planet. God's revelation to Moses starts with an earth covered with water. On day three, we know that the earth was warm enough to keep water soluble and that there was light that enabled the production of plant life before the creation of the sun. On day four the moon, sun and stars superseded the light of the creation on the first day through the third day and whatever kept the earth warm prior to day four.

At the end of the creation on day four Elohim once again says "And the evening and the morning were the fourth day," (Genesis 1:19). In chapter two, I explained this passage in more detail than I will give here. Since the creation of the moon, sun, and stars, a more distinct light has existed that emanates from these celestial bodies. The creation of these celestial bodies gave us a more defined understanding of how Elohim communicated the meaning of day, although there may have been a difference between Elohim's day and ours. Do the days created on day four supersede previously mentioned days when God says, "And the evening and the morning were the fourth day"? It is not likely, because the wording remains the same after each creation day. We cannot overlook that on day four, days and years that existed were more defined because of the creation of the moon, sun, and stars. The days created on day four didn't exist prior to that; the previous days differed, and it was not revealed that the seasons, days, and years existed before day four. It is my observation that the evenings and mornings prior to day four were functioning independent of the lunar seasons, days, and years created on day four. After day four, Elohim was still creating within His own time frame—evening and morning while the seasons, days and years influenced by the moon, sun, and stars, came and went. On day four, the vegetation God created on day three began to perform a more active role in the creation; the earth was prepared for the inhabitation of other forms of life. As we enter day five, the vegetation and celestial bodies Elohim created for food and seasons, has prepared the earth for an exponential creation of life.

He appointed the moon for seasons: the sun knoweth his going down.

(PSALM 104:19)

CHAPTER 6
DAY FIVE

As we enter day five, conditions are ready to sustain life other than vegetation. Day five opens with *"And God said, Let the waters bring forth abundantly the moving creature that hath life, and fowl that may fly above the earth in the open firmament of heaven" (Gen 1:20).* In this passage, Elohim reveals that the first exponential creation of moving creatures came from the waters (seas). This is not surprising since it was revealed that the earth was a watery planet on the first day, and all physical living things need water to survive. On day one it also states that the Holy Spirit was moving (hovering) across the face of the waters. As I stated in chapter two, Elohim is life, and the Holy Spirit is of the person of Elohim. All life comes from God, so if the Holy Spirit was hovering over the waters, I'm sure the Holy Spirit was doing something. As we know, "In the beginning God created the heaven and the earth," which includes life.

The Holy Spirit is God, and He is active in the creation of the heaven and the earth. On the first day, many details in forming the heaven and the earth were absent. Whether God created life in the waters prior to day four may be an enigma, but it is highly conceivable. We know life can exist without sunlight, and the earth was a watery planet that was warm enough to sustain life before the sun was created. The author only reveals to his audience that when life appeared, it was in the form of vegetation on land. The life on land in the form of vegetation was to prepare the way for land animals and fowls of the air. Genesis 1:20 reveals to us that the waters brought forth abundant life. Vegetation had to exist in the waters as well as on land. The creation of plant life was a catalyst to the multiplication of moving creatures and of their kind in the waters. The creation of water creatures and their kind became more complex than the creation of plant life. Genesis 1:20 only reveals that there are moving creatures but doesn't explain what they all were. It could include small to large living things.

On the fifth day Moses chose not to disclose the existence of small microorganisms, or Elohim chose not to reveal them because of their irrelevance to the creation narrative. As John H. Walton stated, "We will assume that although there may be more than the author knew, the truth he did know and communicate was authoritative and inspired."[16] I will also add a passage that is written in the gospel of John, Jesus's beloved disciple: *"And there are also many other things which Jesus did, the which, if they should be written everyone, I suppose that even the world itself could not contain the books that should be written. Amen." (John 21:25).* The omniscience of God is so great that we cannot contain what He knows. The inspired author of Genesis conveys to his audiences a revelation from God with the intent to communicate to them in a way that the creation may be clearly articulated. Though microbes exist, as we know today, it was not important to reveal them to Israel at the time. Victor P. Hamilton's commentary, "The Book of Genesis[17]" makes a correlation between day two and five. He explains how day two brought into existence the necessary environment (the creation of an atmosphere) that the creatures on day five could use to inhabit the sky

---

[16] John H. Walton, Genesis: The NIV Application Commentary, 20.
[17] Victor P. Hamilton, The Book of Genesis Chapter 1-17 (Grand Rapids, Michigan, Wm. B. Eerdmans Publishing, 1990), 129.

and waters—referring to creatures such as birds and aquatic beings. Hamilton then divides the creatures (beings) into two groups: extremely large and smaller. The larger group that was in the waters are mammals (whales, great sea monsters) and large reptiles (crocodiles, large snakes, and great sea monsters). The smaller group consists of smaller fish and tiny aquatic creatures that slide through the water or creep along its beds. Elohim didn't reveal in depth the existence of the diminutive creatures that were in the waters, nor did He discredit their existence. In general, He says, "every living creature that moves." (Genesis 1:21). As Hamilton stated, day two made it necessary for the creatures on day five to inhabit the waters and sky, and infers that smaller life forms could have been created at any time between day two and day five among diminutive creatures such as microbes. As I explained earlier, some microbes do not need sun light to exist and can produce their own food. All life forms need water and oxygen to survive. The world of diminutive creatures is too vast to discuss in this book. God's fundamentals of the creation from day one to day four were needed for the events on the fifth day to occur. The creation narrative was kept simple to communicate to us the order of it.

Genesis 1:20—22 recognizes the creation of life in the flesh among moving creatures and reveals their habitats, which is the waters and the firmaments (skies). In verse 21, Elohim created a difference between moving creatures when He said, *"And God created great whales, and every living creature that moveth, which the waters brought forth abundantly, after their kind, and every winged fowl after his kind: and God saw that it was good." (Gen 1:21)*. It indicates that each living thing that moves was created as a part of a group, separately from other moving things. After He created them after their own kind, he ordered them to reproduce and fill the waters and the seas after their own kind. The command to fill the waters and the seas is an indication that the origin of creation of moving creatures in the waters was localized. Since day four, the waters had been prepared for this expansion of life. Genesis 1:21 also states that God created "great sea creatures." In the original King James Version, it says "great whales." In the Hebrew text, "great whale" is "Tanniyn,"[18] meaning dragon, serpent, and sea monster, which can include dinosaur. Since we know dinosaurs existed, we also can conclude that dinosaurs existed,

---

[18] 2010, Bible Works, Bible Works LLC, BibleWorks9, Norfolk, VA.

as did whales, when moving creatures were created. On day five, Elohim speaks of the life forms He created and commands them to be fruitful and multiply. Though the plants Elohim created on day three were life forms, they weren't as complex as the life-forms on day five. The life-forms on day five had the ability to move at will in the waters and air. Not only did Elohim command them to multiply but He also blessed them that they might fulfill His command. After Elohim created vegetation He said that it was good, but there are no records stating He commanded them to be fruitful and multiply, nor does it say He blessed them. We know they were fruitful because of their ability to produce herbs and fruits. The creation of life on day five has become more defined after moving creatures were created. John H. Walton says in his book, The Lost World of Genesis One,[19] "The contrast to day four of the creation was to support the sphere in which they inhabited." In day five, the creation was to carry out their own function in the cosmic sphere in which they inhabited. On day four, everything's function was to support the ecosystem Elohim created. On day five

---

[19] John H. Walton, The Lost World Of Genesis One (Downer Grove, Il, IVP Academic, 2009), 63.

the function of the birds, whales, fish, and creeping things was to be fruitful and multiply throughout the waters and the air—the environments Elohim had created. These moving creatures utilized the ecosystem to perform Elohim's command with little restrictions—the waters and air were theirs to inhabit.

Life forms on day five were different from any other life forms that previously existed. On day three, Elohim had created plant life, but unlike the life forms on day five, they weren't given the ability to move freely. When plant life was created, the sun wasn't the source of energy for them to produce their own food; the light created on day one was that source. Only when the lunar days were created on day four were they able to utilize the sun for energy to produce their own food. On day five the moving creatures Elohim created were not only able to utilize the energy the sun produced, but also used the lunar day for signs, seasons, days, and years. I agree with Victor P. Hamilton that day two of the creation made it possible for life that moved on day five to exist, although we know that life in the physical form existed on day four and may have existed as far back as day two. It is not to be confused with the eternal life, the life that exists without origin, who is Elohim, the giver of life. Jesus, one of the persons of Elohim, after raising Lazarus from the dead said, *"I am the resurrection, and the life: he that believeth in me, though he were dead, yet shall he live: And whosoever liveth and believeth in me shall never die. Believest thou this?" (John 11:25—26).* In this passage, Jesus is offering believers eternal life (life without death) maybe not in the physical sense as we begin to see it unfold on day five but in the spiritual. God is eternal and is omnipotent and is the creator of all living things. In the creation, we are not talking about the creation of life itself but the creation of life within physical forms. It is highly possible that life in its physical form (life in the flesh) could have been created as far back as day two, life that existed not as vegetation or creeping things, but in the form of microbes. We now know that microbes can exist in areas without sunlight and in extreme temperatures and pressures. I think it is a far stretch to say living things, including microbes, can exist without oxygen and water, although scientists have discovered microbes at the bottom of the Mediterranean in oxygen-free salt water (of the Loriciferans group). Water itself is a chemical compound that is made of two hydrogen atoms and one oxygen atom. Under certain conditions, the hydrogen and oxygen can separate, allowing for a minuscule existence of oxygen in oxygen-free zones, such as where scientists found these forms of microbes. Microbes are essential to life on Earth, so it is safe to say by the time vegetation and moving living things existed, there were microbes. As I said earlier, the world of microbes can be complicated, and the message God wants to convey to us is a simple one. He created the earth to be inhabited by life-forms, and it goes beyond the basic elements of the creation.

Genesis 1:23 once again says, *"And the evening and the morning were the fifth day."* At the end of day five, although the moon, sun, and stars existed, and the seasons, days and years are put in place, Elohim continues His time rather than lunar time to create. From day one to the end of day five, Elohim consistently uses evening and morning at the end of each day, even when the lunar days had been established. It indicates that Elohim's creation was separate from the lunar year. He creates at will according to His time, as on day four. On day five, Elohim's time and lunar time existed together. Elohim was not subject to lunar time; only the life He created was.

So is this great and wide sea, wherein *are* things creeping innumerable, both small and great beasts.

(PSALM 104:25)

CHAPTER 7

DAY SIX

On day six of the creation, other life forms were created that hadn't existed in the waters or the air. Land life-forms were created on this day, such as land mammals and creeping things after their kind, different from the life-forms that were created in the waters and air on day five. On this day, we also see the creation of man and woman which was created to be children of God (Luke 3:38). They were the last to be created and was the most essential to the purpose of God. Day six was the final day of the creation of the Heaven and earth.

On day six Elohim created beast (living animals), "chay" in Hebrew, as an important interrelated part of the earth He created. He further defined some beast as Cattle, "behemah"[20] in Hebrew. In Genesis 1:24 Moses listed behemah (cattle) in-

---

[20] BibleWorks9, NKJ with code, Genesis 1:24.

dependent of chay (living animals), though cattle can be classified as chay when explaining the creation of land animals, but Moses chose to use cattle independently calling them behemah (animals that will most likely gather in groups). The Israelites were nomadic people of origin. When Moses wrote Genesis, cattle was part of their diet as well as using them for spiritual rituals, such as atonement offerings; they were necessary for their survival. One of the major themes of the creation narrative is the creation of life-forms and how these life-forms sustained life. The waters, atmosphere, sea, land, vegetation, and life forms, were all a part of an ecosystem that sustained life. After creating the beasts of the earth, cattle had become an important part of the life cycle for man's survival. In Genesis 4:4, Abel brings the first of his flock, "tse'own" in Hebrew, meaning small cattle such as sheep, goats etcetera, to be offered to God. This offering was a type of atonement that was later offered to God for the forgiveness of sin. Because Abel shed the blood (Hebrew 9:22), the Lord was pleased with Abel's offering. It doesn't say in Genesis 4:4 what type of offering Abel offered in this passage; Genesis 4:2 says Abel was the keeper of sheep. We can assume it was a sheep Abel sacrificed to the Lord—we know the offering pleased God. In the creation day six, tse'own (small cattle) was included with the beast Elohim created. It appeared that Abel knew what animals were to be offered as a sacrifice to God. Later, after the creation, it was written in the books of the Pentateuch (Genesis, Exodus, Leviticus, Numbers, and Deuteronomy) which animals were acceptable for offering. Land life forms had a broader meaning as related to God's acceptance in the use of small cattle for sacrifice and for consumption. It also indicates that man's fall into sin was prescience in the omniscience of Elohim, because Able offered a type of atonement offering from his flock (Genesis 3:7, 21; Hebrews 9:22). Before and after the Fall of man, everything was designed for a purpose. The creation of an ecosystem was needed for life to exist. Each day after the creation Elohim pronounced that it was good, that is, good in design to sustaining the ecosystem and life forms He created in it, with plants as the major provider for food. God said every bird of the air, everything that creeps on the earth, He gives every green herb for food.

> *And to every beast of the earth, and to every fowl of the air, and to everything that creepeth upon the earth, wherein there is life, I have given every green herb for meat: and it was so. (Gen 1:30)*

This passage discloses Elohim's creation of plants, which included trees that yield fruit and herbs that yield seeds for food. In Genesis 3:17—19, after man's fall into sin, God cursed the ground and informed Adam that his ability to produce food from it would be difficult, and it would last until he returned to the ground from which he came. Part of his struggle to produce food would consist of foraging for the herbs of the fields. Elohim made the eating of plant life for survival difficult for him—it would be by the sweat of his brow.

When man was created, he was created from the same ground he would toil with to produce food and would return to after death. But the ground would be different when he returned to it—it would be cursed. Genesis 2:6 describes the place were man was created as a place where the water mist came from the ground to water the earth. Although man may have been created where the mist from the ground covered it, the ground wasn't cursed at that time, only wet and muddy. Genesis 2:7 states that God formed man from the dust of the ground, a watered earth. Although the earth is watered, dust is synonymous with the ground. In Genesis 3:18, God tells Adam that he will return to the ground he was taken from and reminds Adam that he is dust and will return to it. Although the dust can be a product of the ground, during the creation they used them together as one to describe the creation of man, as Job 10:9 explains that God formed him from the dust (ground) like clay and there will be a time when He will return him to the dust.

After man was formed from the dust of the ground, Genesis 2:7 says God breathed into his nostrils the breath of life, and he became a living soul. When man was formed from the dust of the earth, he was given all the physical parts needed to function (brain, eyes, heart, ears etc.), but he was not able to function because there was no life in him; he didn't have a spiritual existence. Then Elohim breathed the breath of life in him, and he became a living soul. The dust he was created from wasn't the soul; it was an instrument designed by Elohim for the soul of man to interact with the physical world around him. The soul is the being of man, created by Elohim prior to man's physical existence. In Jeremiah 1:5, God tells Jeremiah that before He formed him in his mother's womb, He knew him, indicating Jeremiah's soul was conceived long before there was a physical body. When Elohim breathed the breath of life into man, a soul was placed in him, and he had become alive to the material world that the soul may develop. Life comes from God and is eternal. When the soul is placed in the body, it bonds with the body that it may function as a unit. The body cannot exist without the soul but the soul can exist without the body. In the absence of life, the bond between the two are broken, and the body (flesh) returns to the dust, but the soul lives. The Bible tell us in Genesis 35:18 that Rachel had a hard birth, and her soul departed from her in her death. The body cannot live without the soul, and the soul cannot remain in the body without life—life is eternal and comes from God. When God removes the life from the body, the body dies and the soul departs from it. The soul is created by God as a living entity, and it is designed to be eternal; only God can destroy it (Matthew 10:28). In some cases, when we say a person died, we are talking about the soul being absent from the body. There is also a spiritual death. This death doesn't mean that the spirit is destroyed, it is only separated from God.

Man is a tripartite, meaning he consists of three parts: the body, soul, and spirit. The body is the physical part of man. The soul is the conscience, the will, and the emotions.

The spirit of man is that part of him that communicates with God or evil. When the spirit is connected to God, it lives and the soul lives. When the spirit is not connected to God, the soul is considered spiritually dead, causing him to be dependent on his own intellect and are influenced by other spirits that are not of God. If man doesn't allow the spirit of God to guide him, the soul then depend more on intellectually reasoning and becomes more emotionally driven, which in turn affects his conscience and will. When the spirit is dependent on God, the spirit is alive, and therefore the soul is spiritually alive; the soul needs to be connected to a godly spirit to make sound moral judgments. In Genesis 2:17, Elohim forbade man from eating of the tree of knowledge of good and evil, and said if he did, he would die. Elohim was talking about the death of the whole man, the physical body, the soul, and the spirit being separated from God. Man disobeyed God and ate from the tree of knowledge of good and evil; afterward he became morally deficient. He died spiritually first, and eventually he is no longer able to make good moral judgements. Later he dies physically, as God had said he would; he returned to the ground from which he came. When the Bible says, "the soul that sins shall die," it is talking about the death of the whole man. Only by God's grace does He allow life to remain in man. If God removes the life from him, his presence will cease to exist in the physical world. When Jesus says, *"I come to give life that they may have it more abundantly (John 10:10),"* he is talking about restoration—reconnecting spiritually back to God.

Does everything that has life have a soul? The Bible doesn't give us much detail on this topic, but if there is life in the flesh, it most likely has a soul, which would allow the flesh to function in its natural state. God put limitations on how each soul in living things function; some souls are more coherent than others. All things, material or immaterial, are preordained by God—especially living things. Without a soul, the flesh that possess life become inanimate. In the creation, Elohim created a difference between man and all other life-forms. Elohim gave life-forms other than man limited functions to perform, which indicates there is a deficiency of the soul in them. The functions Elohim gave each soul is limited, with mankind soul being far superior to other souls. There is no comparison between the soul of man and any other physical living things—not one. Genesis 1:26 says, "He was created in the image and likeness of God," which makes him far superior to other life-forms. God had not made this claim for any other life-form. To confirm mankind superiority of other life forms He gave man dominion over them (Genesis 1:28). If man has a soul and was created in the likeness and image of God, then God has a soul. Leviticus 26:1—11 tells us that God informs Israel that if they serve Him, He will set His tabernacle among them, and His soul will not abhor them. When Jesus came into the world, He possessed a soul, but it was far superior than any other soul. Hebrews 4:15 tells us that Christ was tempted as we are but didn't sin. This indicates that the soul can be measured. Christ's obedience to God made Him superior to man—His spirit was completely connected to the triune in His earthly vessel. In the creation man was more superior to all other material life-forms and was given dominion over them (Genesis 1:26—28), but they still shared the same ecosystem.

On day five, after the creation of life forms in the sea and air, God blessed them and commanded them to be fruitful and multiply. On day six, after creating life-forms on land, there is no mentioning of God blessing them and commanding them to be fruitful and multiply. Does that mean the land animals were cursed? No, that isn't what is being said. Land, air, and water life-forms that moved and creeped in the earth were different from human life-forms, so they may have been already categorized with all other life-forms a-part from humans. These life-forms are by no means to be compared to the life in man. He was created after the similitude of Elohim, in His likeness and image—he was the son of God. Of all the beasts God paraded before man for him to name them, none was suitable as a mate for him. No ape or any resemblance of the ape, nor that which walked upright which is categorized as prehistoric man was suitable for Adam's mate. As God created man, He also formed his mate using the same pattern. This signifies the superiority of man over all other life-forms. Elohim created his mate from his rib and the dust of the ground. In Luke 3:38, after Jesus had come into the world, Luke traced Jesus's—the Son of God—lineage back to the creation of man. In this passage, Luke says, *"the son of Enos, the son of Seth, the son of Adam, the son of God."* This is a clear indication that man (Adam) wasn't just any life-form; he was the son of God, and his blessings were apart from any other life-form Elohim created.

Day six was the culmination of the creation narrative, with man as Elohim's "prized jewel." He created a life-form that possessed a physical body, soul, and spirit. The tripartite of man is far more complex than these three parts. He was created in the image of God, which includes a conscience, will, emotion, mind, heart, intellect and so forth. Man's attributes give him the ability to adapt to his environment and progress in their thinking that they may know their creator.

And out of the ground the LORD God formed every beast of the field, and every fowl of the air; and brought *them* unto Adam to see what he would call them: and whatsoever Adam called every living creature, that was the name thereof.

(GENESIS 2:19)

CHAPTER 8

DAY SEVEN

On day seven, after the creation of the heaven and earth, the ecosystem created to be inhabited by life-forms was complete. Each life form on land, in the waters, and in the air, had been created after its own kind to be fruitful and multiply on the earth. The stars, sun and moon were formed for seasons, and man—Elohim's "prized jewel," who is created in His image and likeness, for His glory (Isaiah 43:7) and His pleasure (Revelation 4:11) —was given dominion over every living thing that moved upon the earth (water, skies, and land) and over all the earth. The life cycle of the universe was in motion, enabling stars to die while others were born—assisted by the physical laws of the universe created by Elohim. Life forms were created to regenerate on the earth (John 12:24) as the seasons came and went. Even man, designed to be eternal, at an acceptable time, would be transformed from flesh and blood into the Kingdom of

God (Genesis 5:24). Genesis 1:1, summarizes the creation from day one through day six. Genesis 2:1 is like Genesis 1:1 but summarizes the creation while putting more emphasis on the finishing of the creation, noting the host of the heaven and earth too signifying that the substances of the universe were created in a uniform order for the purpose for which they were created.

Day seven makes no mention of the evenings and morning, as previous days did. At the end of each evening and morning of a creation period, the next creation period began, but it doesn't say God rested. The time Elohim used to create the heaven and the earth was completed on day six. The universe that is set in motion after the terrestrial and extraterrestrial bodies were created becomes a type of Elohim's periods of time, or days. The time-period Elohim created on day four became fully active and noticeable on day seven. From there on, it continues without rest. After the completion of each evening and morning, it doesn't say Elohim rested; it only says, "evening and the morning" of that day before advancing into the next day. It is an indication that each day was created for a purpose, and when that purpose was complete, Elohim advanced to the next purpose—time existed but wasn't the major factor. Only on day seven does it say Elohim rested. On day seven, there was no more creation of the heaven and the earth as disclosed in the book of Genesis—Elohim rested, calling it the seventh day: the Sabbath. In the Hebrew lexicon, the accepted word most commonly used for rest is sabath (sabbath), meaning to cease. Rather than saying Elohim rested, it meant he ceased or finished the creation of the Genesis heaven and the earth. This was a special day because Elohim had finished the works of the creation, and sanctified it (Genesis 2:1—3). Later, God informed Israel that the seventh day was for their keeping—it was sanctified (holy), and on the Sabbath only there was no work to be performed—it became a holy day of rest for them. At the end of day six, Elohim said, "It is good," but the seventh day He sanctified. As written in the Ten Commandments (Exodus 20:8—11, 35:2), He commands Israel to remember it and keep it sanctified (holy). God explains to them that in six days He created the heavens and the earth and rested the seventh day and blessed it and made it hallowed. On that day, Israel, strangers within their gates, and beasts of burden were not to do any work. It was to be a type of God's rest after finishing the creation of the heaven and the earth. It allowed them to rest from carnal labor after six days of work, and after honoring the sabbath they would return once again to their carnal labor.

The seventh day has a twofold meaning. It is holy (as a memorial) to Elohim's rest from the works of His creation (Genesis 2:1-3) and as a day of rest for Israel. In Exodus 16:23—29, God commands Israel to keep the Sabbath holy, because it is sanctified. Therefore, He required them to do all work the days prior, because it is a day to be honored as a day of rest to honor His rest. Moses explained to Israel that not only was the Sabbath a memorial to God's rest after His creation work, but it was also designed for His people that they might have rest after their labor, it had become a law for them. When they honor the Sabbath day they honor God, and the keeping of His law. God signifies the importance of the keeping of the seventh day (Sabbath) by placing it in the Ten Commandment. He writes:

> *Remember the Sabbath day, to keep it holy. Six days you shall labor and do all your work, but the seventh day is the Sabbath of the Lord your God. In it you shall do no work: you, nor your son, nor your daughter, nor your male servant, nor your female servant, nor your*

cattle, nor your stranger who is within your gates. For in six days the Lord made the heavens and the earth, the sea, and all that is in them, and rested the seventh day. Therefore, the Lord blessed the Sabbath day and hallowed it. (Exodus 20:8—11 NKJV)

The Sabbath is more than a day of rest. It is a memorial to an omnipotent and omniscient God who created all things. To say that the Ten Commandments are no longer relevant is to dishonor the Creator of the heaven and the earth and the memorial to His rest in creating them. In the Ten Commandments, not only did God speak of the Sabbath but also the creation of the heavens and the earth. They didn't come into existence by any other means—Elohim was the Creator. Also in the Commandments God warns us against recognizing any other thing as the creator of all things and letting us know that if we do this, it is a demonstration of hate toward Him, and if we recognize Him as the creator, it is a demonstration of love toward Him. In Exodus 20:5—6 God writes:

You shall not bow down to them nor serve them. For I, the Lord your God, am a jealous God, visiting the iniquity of the fathers on the children to the third and fourth generations of those who hate Me, but showing mercy to thousands, to those who love Me and keep My commandments. (NKJV)

Does God Need Rest?

We know that God doesn't need physical rest because He is a spirit and not flesh and blood. Only flesh and blood requires physical rest. In Isaiah 40:28, Isaiah prophesies to Judah of their impending exile. He reminds them of who God is and lets them know that there are no limits to His power. He explains that God doesn't faint (get fatigued) or get weary. Because of this, He gives power to the weak and gives strength to those who have no might. Revelation 4:8 speaks of four living creatures around the throne of God crying, "Holy, holy, holy"—never resting, never tiring. Since God is the Creator and is greater than these four creatures, we know that God needs no rest as they needed no rest. The rest God is talking about in Genesis 2:2, is not a rest from fatigue. Here Elohim was saying that He ceased the work of the creation of the heaven and the earth on the seventh day (Sabbath). There was no mentioning that Elohim took rest after the creation of each evening and morning (day), indicating He is an untiring God. Genesis 2:2 is not speaking of an exhausted God who needed rest after working but the designer and creator of the universe. He is sovereign and finishes what He starts and then ceases from it. In this case, it was the creation of the heaven and the earth and the life forms that inhabited it—that is what He ceased from.

Is There Another Rest?

Jesus said, *"I must work the works of Him who sent Me while it is day; the night is coming when no one can work" (John 9:4 NKJ)*. Jesus explains that He was sent to do a work and must do it while it is day because when the night comes He can no longer perform the work He was sent to do. At this point, the work Jesus was sent to perform in the flesh had not been physically completed. The work spoken of in the book of Genesis in Hebrew is *mela'kah*,[21] and in John 9:4 it is written in Greek as *"ergazomai"*[22]—both have the same meaning concerning work. In Genesis, Elohim rested from *mela'kah* (work), but in John 9:4, *ergazomai* (work) continues after the coming of night for Jesus and will continue until He return. The night represented Jesus's death, burial,

---

[21] BibleWorks9, NKJV with code, Genesis 2:2.
[22] BibleWorks9, NKJV with code, John 9:4.

resurrection, and ascension. In Genesis 2:2, Elohim rested from His creation—work—and established the Sabbath as a memorial to it. In John 9:4, the work continues even after the glorification of Jesus (His resurrection). The resurrection of Jesus Christ reveals another rest, not a rest from carnal labor but a spiritual rest. The carnal rest in Genesis 2:2 is a type of the spiritual rest mentioned in John: 9:4, which is a rest for the soul—a rest from the law of sin and death.

Come unto me, all ye that labor and are heavy laden, and I will give you rest. Take my yoke upon you, and learn of me; for I am meek and lowly in heart: and ye shall find rest unto your souls. For my yoke is easy, and my burden is light. (Matt. 11:28—30)

In these passages, Jesus is not talking about a Sabbath rest from physical labor but a rest for the soul. This rest can only come through taking on the yoke of Jesus Christ, and that yoke is His teaching—the Word of God. Applying the teaching of Christ in our lives frees us from the bondage of sin and the law. Both Genesis 2:2 and John 9:4 refer to work, but Genesis 2:2 is a reference to a finished work, and the Sabbath was established as a memorial to that rest—the work of the creation was finished, and Elohim rested.

The work mentioned in John 9:4 continues from generation to generation and becomes a rest for the individual who takes on the yoke of Jesus Christ. In Matthew 28:18—20, Jesus says to His disciples, *"All authority has been given to Me in heaven and on earth. Go therefore and make disciples of all the nations, baptizing them in the name of the Father and of the Son and of the Holy Spirit, "teaching them to observe all things that I have commanded you; and lo, I am with you always, even to the end of the age."* With authority from above, Jesus commands His disciples to make disciples, baptizing them in the name of the Triune, and teach them the same gospel he was sent to teach. Though no longer in the flesh, through the Holy Spirit He will be with them to the end of the age, through the Holy Spirit the day (light) returns and Jesus once again can be seen as the visible light of the world. The work Jesus was sent to do is continues until the end of the age. This work is given to those who take the yoke of Jesus Christ—the church—those who are called out to spread the gospel of Jesus Christ.

The rest Jesus speaks of existed long before His coming—it was in the foreknowledge of God before it was finished on the cross by Jesus. The Sabbath day was a type of the rest Jesus gave us; rather than a rest from carnal labor, it is a rest from the bondage of sin and all of its burdens. The rest through Jesus Christ continues to this day because Jesus had victory over sin by enduring the cross. Hebrew, 12:2 says, *"Looking unto Jesus, the author and finisher of our faith, who for the joy that was set before Him endured the cross, despising the shame, and has sat down at the right hand of the throne of God."* The rest from sin and its burdens written about in John 9:4 was planned in the prescience of God, and was completed by the work of the cross through Jesus Christ. As it is written, *"All who dwell on the earth will worship him, whose names have not been written in the Book of Life of the Lamb slain from the foundation of the world" (Rev 13:8 NKJV).* Those who received His rest, their names are written in the book of Life of the Lamb (Jesus Christ), and nothing can stop this because it was finished on the cross. Those who reject Jesus will recognize Him in judgement. In John 19:30, Jesus testifies while on the cross the work He was sent to do was finished by saying, "It is finished." Jesus told His disciples that the gates of hell would not prevent the gospel of the kingdom from spreading (Matthew 16:18). The prescience of God is not like man's predictions—God's prescience is real and will not falter. It will come to pass—it is already done and will come to fruition. According to John 5:36, the work Jesus was sent to do must come to fruition before we are to be delivered from sin, and for Jesus to be glorified. After the night came, Jesus had the victory over sin and was glorified—because Jesus went to His father. His death and resurrection ushered in a greater work.

If Jesus ushered in a greater work, then there must be a greater rest than the Sabbath of Genesis 2:2. Believers could only perceive the carnal rest of the Sabbath until Jesus gave them a greater rest. God being omniscient, knew that because of free will, Satan and his demons would rebel and bring the yoke of the bondage of sin upon a free man who chose to disobey God. Because of disobedience, man had lost rest for his soul. Genesis 6:5 says, *"Then the Lord saw that the wickedness of man was great in the earth, and that every intent of the thoughts of his heart was only evil continually."* There was no rest from sin because they had forsaken their creator. Because of this, evil increased, and God sent a flood to destroy those who practiced it.

Jesus explained to His disciples that He would not leave them helpless (comfortless) and that in His name the Father would send them another helper (John 14:26). He would guide them into truth and would not speak of His own authority but of that which was spoken through Jesus Christ (John 16:13). In John 14:12, Jesus tells those that believe in Him that they will do greater work, which is to preach the gospel of Jesus Christ to the whole world so that those who are called out can take His yoke and learn of Him to find rest for their souls. Jesus said, *"But you shall receive power when the Holy Spirit has come upon you; and you shall be witnesses to Me in Jerusalem, and in all Judea and Samaria, and to the end of the earth." (Act 1:8 NKJV)*. The helper (comforter) who comes in the name of Jesus will empower His disciples—the church—with the ability to spread the gospel of Jesus throughout the whole world with a lessened burden and an easy yoke. The ceremonial and the civil parts of the law were fulfilled in Jesus Christ—only the moral part of the law remained. The blood of Jesus had cleansed believers from all unrighteousness. The Sabbath is a type of rest Jesus finished on the cross, although sin hadn't been introduced into the world by Satan through Adam and Eve when the Sabbath was instituted. In the prescience of God, there was a need for a greater rest. The creation of the heaven and the earth along with the Sabbath, was a prelude to the great commission calling for the world to enter God's rest—a rest of the soul.

Does God Still Create?

The Bible doesn't clearly reveal if God is still creating. There is an assumption that since Elohim finished creating the heaven and the earth, there is nothing else to be created. Psalm 102:18 writes of a people who shall be created that will praise the Lord. In this passage, created in Hebrew is "bara'."[23] It is the same translation used for created in Genesis 1:1, where it says, "In the beginning God created the heaven and the earth." In Genesis 1:1, created, "bara'," is used to indicate that Elohim brought into existence the heaven and the earth from that which didn't exist—a supernatural event. Psalm 102:18 also uses "bara'" when it say created, although the people that shall be created are not from nonexistence, as was the heaven and the earth in Genesis 1:1, because there was already a formal existence prior to their creation as descendants of Adam. If Psalm 102:18 was physical talking about a creation of a people from nonexistence, it can be construed that the people created in Psalm 102 was not subject to the original sin of Adam. The Bible doesn't tell us that. It says, *"Wherefore, as by one man sin entered into the world, and death by sin;*

---

[23] BibleWorks9, KJV with code, Geneses 1:1.

and so death passed upon all men, for that all have sinned:" (Rom 5:12), indicating that all of mankind is born after the original sin of Adam, including those written of in Psalm 102:18. It is not disclosing the recreation of man again but rather the creation of a new people that are redeemed by God through His Son into His image and likeness, a regenerated people from the old man Adam, they knew sin but they rejected the practice of it and chose to be reconciled to God through Jesus Christ by the indwelling of the Holy Spirit. Jesus's glorification created a people that became the children of God, freed (by choice) from the yoke of sin by taking on the yoke of Jesus Christ. By taking on His yoke, they will be like Him. After Jesus's glorification, He could appear and disappear at will (Luke 24:31, John 20:19) and able to ascend into heaven (Mark 16:19). The beauty of it all is that we shall be like Him (1 John 3:2). In this sense, created, "bara," in Psalm 102:18 can be used as Genesis 1:1 created because the people created in Psalm 102:18 were nonexistent prior to their creation, and it is supernatural like Genesis 1:1.

Another debate about whether God is still creating, is the creation of a new heaven and new earth as written in

Revelation 21:1. The defense of this argument depends on whether you view this passage literally or symbolically. The symbolic argument is that God is a reconciliation God; therefore, He will restore the earth rather than destroy it. It is said the new heaven and the new earth are the same earth as it is at present and as in the creation account of Genesis. In Revelation 21:1, where it says, "there were no more seas," they argues that its meaning is symbolic rather than literal. The seas are interpreted to be turmoil and chaos, and the absence of them means there would be no more turmoil in the new earth. I agree that there will be no more turmoil in the new earth, but the rest of the argument cannot be plausible if there is a belief in the veracity of the sixty-six books of the Bible. Second Peter 3:12 states that the heaven and the earth will be dissolved and the elements will melt away. Some theologians argue against this passage and feel it shouldn't be a part of the Bible, but the early church proved this passage to be authentic and canonized the New Testament, including 2 Peter, at the councils at Hippo in 393 and later ratified it in 397 at Carthage.[24] In Isaiah 34:4,

---

[24] Everett Ferguson, Church History: From Christ to Pre-Reformation, Volume One (Grand Rapids, Michigan, Zondervan, 2005), 117.

God reveals His indignation upon the nation, the earth, and the heavens, where it is said He will dissolve the heavens.

If Revelation 21:1 is interpreted literally, we see on the seventh day of Genesis 2:2—3, Elohim rests from the creation work of the first "heaven and the earth." In Revelation 21:1, the Apostle John sees a new heaven and new earth and explains that the first earth had passed away. The new heaven and new earth created after the first were different in many ways. There will be no more seas, there will be living water (Revelation 7:17), there will be no sun, and darkness will not exist (Isaiah 65:17; Revelation 21:23, 22:5). This can be construed that there is a creation of a new heaven and earth. Being that it is in the future, it is possible that its creation is after the Genesis heaven and earth creation. Revelation 21:1 should be taken literally. Although it was in the prescience of God, He created a people unlike any other people to inhabit that new heaven and new earth, bringing that which is prescience to fruition. The rest of the newly created people spoken of in Psalm 102:18 was a rest unlike any other rest mentioned in the Bible. It is a rest from sin and all that is symbolic to it. Adam was not capable of giving us this rest, because of his sinful nature. Only one without sin can deliver us from it that we may enter His rest. Jesus Christ, the only begotten Son of God, was the fulfillment of the symbolic sacrificial laws for God to create a people that would be free from sin and would serve and praise Him freely, untiring like the creatures around the throne of God and the heavenly hosts.

It *is* a sign between me and the children of Israel for ever: for *in* six days the LORD made heaven and earth, and on the seventh day he rested, and was refreshed.

(EXODUS 31:17)

CONCLUSION

The Bible is the progressive revelation of the truth about God. Through it, God communicates to mankind the mystery of who He is and the purpose of our existence. In it, the creator reveals His being, His moral and non-moral divine attributes, and the purpose of His creation. In the creation of the heaven and the earth, Elohim doesn't reveal the creation of all things, only the creation of the heaven and the earth. There Elohim enters time and space to create them. In the creation, Elohim reveals to us the existence of time and space and uses them to create the heaven and the earth in periods of time rather than all at once. Elohim calls these periods of times "evening and morning." Time enables mankind to know God through progressive revelation. Through time, God reveals His being and confirms the truth of His creation. When Moses writes in Genesis 1:1, "In the beginning God created the heaven and the earth," he was not revealing the creation of time and space, but it is the revelation of their existence in the creation. Elohim, who is transcendent, moves in and out of time and space to create the heaven and the earth. The Holy Spirit hovered over the waters as time advanced. The angels rejoiced as they witnessed an omnipotent, omniscient, and sovereign God create the heavens and the earth. Moses revealed the truth of the creation in the book of Genesis and the Ten Commandments, and God confirms this truth throughout the progression of time. Isaiah 42:5 proclaims that the Lord is the creator of the heavens and the earth, and announces the coming of the Messiah (Isaiah 7:14, 9:6—7). The Apostle John reveals that Jesus was in the beginning and was of the Triune that made all things (John 1:1—3), and the Apostle John reveals the revelation of the creation, that God created the heaven and the earth within time and that the time for humanity will soon end. The word of God gives veracity to the creation of the heaven and the earth. On day one we see the revelation of time and space, the creation of the waters and the land under the waters and light in the presence of the Holy Spirit.

How do we know what is written concerning the creation is true? God is visibly active in history, using different inspired authors to reveal to us that Elohim is the God of the creation. To ensure the veracity of His truth, He guarantees the survival of the scriptures no matter the calamities that come upon them that teach it. In the Old Testament, God communicates to the believers through the writings of the Pentateuch, history, poetry, wisdom, and prophesy. In the New Testament, God communicates with His believers through the teaching of Jesus Christ and the Apostles through the Holy Spirit, which include the Gospels, Acts of the Apostles, the Epistles, Prophesy and the Old Testament. These forms of communication are what God uses to inform the faithful that He is alive and is active in the affairs of men—He is sovereign. He is not a distant or unparticipating God, but He reveals himself in a time of need to ensure the faith of the believers. In the New Testament, God becomes indwelling, guaranteeing the faith of the believers to the end of time. In Matthew 16:18, Jesus tells us that He will build His church and that the gates of Hell will not prevail against it. This proclamation of Jesus Christ ensures the veracity of the Word of God, and reveals its absolute truth.

Some may say the mind cannot comprehend the concept of absolute truth because we are egocentric and it influences the mind enabling us to think more subjectively. God confirms this assessment of mankind's dependence on subjectively thinking. In Isaiah 55:8—9, God tells Israel that their thoughts are not His thoughts or their ways His ways. If we rely solely on how we perceive things through life experiences, we become subjective in thinking. There are many things that can cause us to be subjective and prevent us from knowing the truth of God: wealth, poverty, death, sickness, tragedy, desires and more. Subjective thinking can cause us to resist the truth and turn from it. If we are unable to comprehend absolute truth, we become dependent on reason and that what appears to be true. Proverb 14:12 tell us that there is a way that seems right to us but the end of it is death. Although some say there is more than one truth, there is only one absolute truth, and it exists whether we believe it or not—it will always be truth. God reveals to us in the Scriptures that His Words are absolute. In Matthew 24:35, Jesus tells His disciples that heaven and Earth will pass away, but His Word will always exist. Jesus is informing us that the truths of this world are not absolute, when the heaven and Earth pass away, they, too, will pass. Although mankind thinks subjectively, the Word of God enables us to think less subjectively in order to find truth that we may know the Creator. Because of subjective reasoning some will say there is no Creator of the heaven and earth. Apostle John said Jesus was in the beginning and created all things—he is the Word of God. In John 14:6, Jesus tells His disciples that He is the way, the truth, and the life, and no man comes to the Father except by Him. Jesus also tells believers that knowing the truth, will set us free (John 8:31—32). Truth without God breeds war, oppression, hatred, greed, murder, obsession, addiction, and all other ills of society.

To grasp the absolute truth, we don't need to be proficient in understanding science, have wealth or power, or to be highly intelligent. To obtain the absolute truth we must know that God, our Creator exists, submit to Him, learn of Him and follow His teachings. Jesus, the creator of the heaven and earth, who was in the beginning, and is of the Triune, came into the world that we may know the truth that we may implement it in our lives to free us from the destructive nature of sin. The absolute truth of God always exists. God created the heavens and the earth that mankind will know the truth concerning His non-moral and moral attributes, that one day believers will become the children of God.

God was fully aware that mankind would fall into sin, but through progressive revelation, He redeemed mankind from sin. God revealed to Moses His presence in creating the heaven and the earth as the Holy Spirit hovered over the face of the waters, laying the foundation of the creation of life-forms. The truth to Elohim's presence in the creation of the heavens and the earth is manifested. Elohim (Father, Son, Holy Spirit) is life and the giver of it. Jesus informs us that the Father is life in John 5:26; John 14:6 reveals that Jesus is life; 2 Corinthians 3:6, Paul reveals that the Holy Spirit is life; and in Revelation 11:11, the Apostle John also reveals to us that the Holy Spirit is life. The Spirit of life that existed on day one was there to prepare the earth for inhabitation, especially for His most "prized jewel," mankind, the sons of God (Luke 3:38).

Day one revealed Elohim as the creator of light, and that only He knows the mystery of it, from its beginning to its end. He revealed to us the existence of time and space and how He uses them to create the heaven and the earth. On this day, He also created water, the sustainer of life-forms. The first day was the cornerstone of the creation of the heaven and the earth. It laid the foundation for the forming of the earth to sustain life forms. Elohim is saying to us, I am sovereign and possess all authority; I am omniscient, knowing all things; I am omnipotent and can do all things at will from that which I know.

Day two furthers the advancement of forming the earth for habitation. Elohim separates the waters, creating a firmament between them; He called the firmament "sky." The sky was also created to sustain life forms that the earth could be inhabited. On day three, Elohim divided the water by causing dry land to appear. Dry land is used in the creation to sustain the first visible form of life (vegetation). The first order of life-forms Elohim revealed to us created on this day was grass, herbs, and fruit-bearing trees. This vegetation utilized the nutrients from the light, water, sky and land to exist. On this day, the earth had been prepared for the exponential creation of other life-forms. On day four, the moon, sun, and stars were created for signs and seasons. Here we can visualize the cosmos in motion and the cycle of time and life through the changing of the seasons, day and night, and the yielding of seeds and fruits as the seasons came and went. On the fifth day, Elohim reveals the creation of life-forms in the waters and air. Although he didn't describe in detail how many life forms were created on this day, we know it was vast, from the creation of great whales (dragons, serpents, and sea monsters) and fowls of the air, to the creation of small aquatic creatures that lived and moved in the seas. For every living thing in the waters that moved and every winged fowl, it is revealed that God created them on this day. On the sixth day, God revealed the creation of land animals, cattle, and beasts of the field, which included dinosaurs (behemoth). Elohim revealed to Moses that everything that moved upon the earth, great or small, was created by Him. This included mankind, Elohim's most "prized jewel," who is created in His "image and likeness."

From Adam to Moses, the account of the creation has been both objective and subjective. There are many accounts of the creation, but only one of them are true. In the ancient Near East, there are accounts of the creation from the Israelites, Babylonian, Sumerians, Canaanites, Egyptians and others. Since there is only one truth, which account of the creation is correct? God communicated to us through historical time events His plan for mankind so that we may know who He is. The more we comprehend who God is, the better we know Him. As God communicates with us, He reveals to us the truthfulness of His word in Scripture by demonstrating His sovereignty throughout history to let us know that He is faithful to His word. As the creation of Heaven and the earth was designed in the foreknowledge of God, so also is His plan for mankind. In the Scripture, He revealed to Abraham that his seed will be afflicted in a strange land for four hundred years, then He would judge the inhabitants of that land and bring them out of the land with great substance (Genesis 15:13—14); God informed Ezekiel that after the scattering of Israel into other countries because of their ungodly rulers, He will later bring them back into their land from the countries where they were scattered (Ezekiel 34:10—13); God informs Isaiah that a virgin will give birth to the son of God (Isa. 7:14); Matthew informs us that the son of God will bring salvation to believers (Matthew 1:21); Jesus told His disciples that a comforter will come in His name, He will teach and bring to remembrance whatsoever He told them (Matthew 14:26; John 16:13; Acts 2: 1—4); Jesus tells us that the comforter is the Spirit of truth (John 16:13), He will testify of Jesus Christ (John 15:26) and will help us walk in the truth (John 16:13) that we may become children of God (Romans 8:16-17). These are the promises of a true and living God that came to pass. Throughout historical time periods God revealed Himself to us and continues to do so today. The gods of Israel's Near Eastern neighbors were inanimate and did not communicate with their people as did the God of Abraham, Isaac, Jacob, the Apostles, the church and the world. Israel's Near Eastern neighbor's gods no longer exist today. There was no personal relationship with those who served them, neither did they walk among them in love as did the creator of the heaven and the earth. To this day, the God of Israel, the Apostles, the church and the world exist. He is the only true and living God, and continues to intercede into the affairs of mankind. God interceding in the affairs of mankind give truth to the creation account of Moses because it was revealed to him by God.

God created a garden as a dwelling place for Adam and Eve, and forbade them from seeking knowledge from the tree that would open the eyes to good and evil. Eve disobeyed God, ate from the fruit of the tree, and encouraged Adam to do so as well. In their disobedience, they obtained knowledge of good and evil but truth became a casualty to them. It was inevitable that in time, the truth about the creation would be distorted.

> *"Because that, when they knew God, they glorified him not as God, neither were thankful; but became vain in their imaginations, and their foolish heart was darkened. Professing themselves to be wise, they became fools, and changed the glory of the uncor-*

ruptible God into an image made like to corruptible man, and to birds, and four-footed beasts, and creeping things. Wherefore God also gave them up to uncleanness through the lusts of their own hearts, to dishonour their own bodies between themselves: Who changed the truth of God into a lie, and worshipped and served the creature more than the Creator, who is blessed forever." (Rom 1:21-25)

Paul informs us of why the truth has been distorted. Mankind knew God but rejected Him and became unthankful. Paul understood Scripture because of the progressive revelation of God revealed to him through historical events. After mankind fell from grace, God offered redemption through His Son, Jesus Christ. Throughout history, God increases the revelation of the truth to man, that he would better understand God's redemption for him; as we become more versed in the truth, it enables us to know our Creator better.

The creation of the heaven and the earth became the foundation for the events that are to come. After the creation, Elohim rested on the seventh day from the work of the creation. All things thereafter had been set in motion.

In time, believers would know the truth and overcome the bondage of sin because of the fall into sin by Adam and Eve and our subjective reasoning. God, the great communicator, reveals the truth to us down through history, and when Jesus came into the world, many understood His truth, despite our subjective thoughts. From the creation to Jesus Christ and the Apostles, He reveals the truth to mankind that we may know it. Through the revelation of the truth in historical times, God brings us back to Him through the generations of mankind, demonstrating His attributes that we may know Him. God chose Abraham and his descendants to reintroduce the truth to mankind. Eventually this culminated on the day of Pentecost through the outpouring of the Holy Spirit, whom the Father sends in the name of Jesus Christ. The coming of the Holy Spirit gives abundant life to believers that they may become the children of God.

In John 17:5, when Jesus was aware that the time of His crucifixion was near, He discloses that He is a person of Elohim and was in the beginning of the creation. Jesus prayed to the Father that He would be once again glorified as before the creation of the world. It was planned before the beginning of the creation that He would be the sacrificial lamb to redeem mankind; it is the revelation of a just God. After Jesus's death and resurrection, He was to return to the Triune in glory, as He was before the creation. Jesus's resurrection revealed the truth that in the beginning God created the heaven and the earth. The greater purpose of the creation was fulfilled in Jesus Christ that those who believe in Him become the children of God. After the creation, Elohim rested on the seventh day, and God's purpose for mankind was complete but had not yet come to fruition. God revealed to Moses, Israel and us the truth in creating the heaven and the earth. Although many reject this account of the creation, it remains true.

The God of Israel was unlike any other god. He communicated with His creation for us to know His being. Mankind was so important to Him that the revelation of the truth had become progressive through historical time so that eventually those who believe in Him will understand and know their Creator and their purpose. The truth existed before the creation of the heavens and the earth in the foreknowledge of God. In Mark 10:6, Jesus states that before the creation, God made male and female, signifying that their creation was planned before the existence of the cosmos.

For thus saith the Lord that created the heavens; God himself that formed the earth and made it; he hath established it, he created it not in vain, he formed it to be inhabited: I am the Lord; and there is none else. (Isaiah 45:18)

Isaiah revealed the word of the Lord to Israel that He didn't create the heaven and the earth in vain. It was planned to be created and to be inhabited. God proclaims that there is none like Him. The God of Israel and of the Apostles are one and the same, and is the only God. He is the true and living God. Though the gods of Israel's Near Eastern neighbors no longer exist, the God of Abraham, Israel, and the Apostles is alive and is active in the events of the world. To prevent the distortion of the truth, God sent the Holy Spirit to indwell believers as a testimony to Jesus Christ that we may be witnesses unto Him (John 15:26—27). Jesus said the Holy Spirit, the Spirit of Truth, would guide believers to the truth and reveal to them the things to come (John 16:13).

The creation of the heaven and the earth to some is a fable because it is inconceivable to them that a supernatural

God exists. They believe that if it can't be proven, it doesn't exist. However, God has proven throughout time through historical events of the Bible that He exists. His existence is proven every day. God is full of wisdom and knows that in the last days, there will be an aggressive attack on the faith of His believers. He sent the Holy Spirit—the Spirit of Truth that those who believe in Him will know He exists no matter how dark things get. The Holy Spirit, is the same Spirit that hovered over the face of the waters in the creation and today is the witness to the truth (John 15:26). The creation of the heaven and the earth by Elohim is the absolute truth no matter how great the distortion of it exists among unbelievers in the world today. The Holy Spirit revealed to Paul that there will be those who follow their own imaginations and disrespected God.

To those who believe we must always be true to Genesis 1:1: "In the beginning God created the heaven and the earth." To those who seek truth, come into the Body of Christ (the church), receive his spirit and study the Bible that you may learn of our Creator who created the heaven and the earth, Amen.

Many, O LORD my God, *are* thy wonderful works *which* thou hast done, and thy thoughts *which are* to us-ward: they cannot be reckoned up in order unto thee: *if* I would declare and speak *of them*, they are more than can be numbered.

(PSALM 40:5)

BIBLIOGRAPHY

1. Alexander, T. Desmond and David W. Baker, ed. Dictionary of the Old Testament Pentateuch: A Compendium of Contemporary Biblical Scholarship. Downer Grove, Illinois: InterVarsity Press, 2003. Kindle

2. BibleWorks 9. Software for Biblical Exegesis and Research: www.bibleworks.com. Norfolk, Virginia: BibleWorks LLC, 2010.

3. Carson D. A. The Gospel According To John. Grand Rapids, Michigan: Wm. B. Eerdmans Publishing, 1991.

4. Feinberg, John S., ed. No One Like Him: The Doctrine of God. Wheaton, Illinois: Crossway, 2001.

5. Ferguson, Everett. Church History Volume One: From Christ to Pre-Reformation. Grand Rapids, Michigan: Zondervan, 2005.

6. Groothuis, Douglas. Christian Apologetics: A Comprehensive Case for Biblical Faith. Downer Grove, Illinois: InterVarsity Press USA, 2011.

7. Hamilton, Victor P. The Book Of Genesis Chapters 1-17: The New International Commentary on the Old Testament. Wm. B. Eerdmans Publishing, 1990.

8. Lockyer, Herbert. All the Angels in the Bible. Peabody, Massachusetts: Henderson Publishers, Inc, 1995.

9. Merrill, Eugene H., Mark F. Rooker and Michael A. Grisanti. The World And The Word: An Introduction to the Old Testament. Nashville, Tennessee: B&H Publishing Group, 2011.

10. Oswalt, John N. The Bible Among the Myths: Unique Revelation of Just Ancient Literature. Grand Rapids, Michigan: Zondervan, 2009.

11. Oswalt, John N. Isaiah: The NIV Application Commentary. Grand Rapids, Michigan: Zondervan, 2003.

12. Schaeffer, Francis A. Genesis in Space and Time. Downer Grove, Illinois: InterVarsity Press, 1972.

13. Scientific American, ed. Evolution vs Creationism: Inside the Controversy. New York, NY: Scientific American Publisher, 2017. Kindle.

14. Snoke, David. A Biblical Case for an Old Earth. Grand Rapids, Michigan: Baker Books, 2006.

15. Stanley Steven M. Earth System History: Fourth Edition. New York, NY: W. H. Freeman and Company, 2015.

16. Walton, John, H. Ancient Near Eastern Thoughts and the Old Testament: Introducing the Conceptual World of the Hebrew Bible. Grand Rapids, MI: Baker Academic, 2006.

17. Walton, John H. Genesis: The NIV Application Commentary. Grand Rapids, Michigan: Zondervan, 2001.

18. Walton, John, H. The Lost World of Genesis One: Ancient Cosmology and the Origins Debate. Downer Grove, Illinois: InterVarsity Press, 2009.

19. Walton, John, H., Victor H. Mathews and Mark W, Chavalas. The IVP Bible Background Commentary: Old Testament. Downer Grove, Illinois: InterVarsity Press, 2000. Kindle.

20. Whitcomb, John C. The Genesis Flood: The Biblical Records and Its Scientific Implications. Phillipsburg, New Jersey: P&R Publishing, 2011.

INDEX OF SCRIPTURES

Genesis

1:1	7, 8, 17, 18, 19, 20, 21, 23, 100, 111, 112, 117, 131
1:2	15, 23, 24, 25, 27, 28, 29, 30, 32, 33, 34, 41, 42, 57, 58, 74
1:3-4	31
1:5	35, 36, 38, 42, 44
1:6-8	47, 48, 49, 54, 55
1:10	24, 25, 27
1:9-10	58
1:14	68, 73
1:16	73
1:18	40
1:19	74
1:21	80, 81
1:20-22	81
1:23	85
1:24	87

1:26	15, 18, 94, 95
1:26-28	95
1:29	29, 64
1:30	89
2:1-3	101, 102
2:2	104, 105, 106, 109, 114
2:4-5	66
2:4-6	66
2:7	90, 91
3:7, 21	89
3:17-19	90
4:4	88
5:1	18
5:21-24	21
6:5	18, 109
6:13	18
6:15	59
6:17	25
7:4	50
7:11-12	25
7:12	25
7:19	26, 48
7:21	25
7:22	27

8:5	26
8:7	27
9:1	18
10:1	18
10:6	18
1:11-12	66
14:19	10
15:13-14	125
15:2	10
18:1-3	20
19:1	20
26:4	50
35:18	92

Exodus

3:6-7	3
3:13-15	16
6:3	11, 16
19:9	3
10:21-23	33
13:3-4	71
14:19	20, 33
14:21-22, 29	61
14:22	61

20:6	103
20:11	18
20:8-11	101, 103
33:20	21
35:2	101

Numbers
12:1-14	3
12:7-8	18
21:5	30

Deuteronomy
6:4	16
11:15	64
34:10	66
16:9-11	69

Joshua
4:18, 22	61

Judges
13:17-18	20

1 Kings
8:27	51
8:30	52

2 Chronicles
7:14	12

Job
10:9	91
10:11-12	29
38:4-7	20

Psalm
36:9	29
82:8	16
102:18	111, 112, 114
148:2, 5	20, 43

Ecclesiastes
3:11	38
12:7	29

Isaiah
6:2-6	37
6:3	24
7:14	118, 125
9:6-7	118
43:7	12, 99
14:12-14	20

24:18	
34:4	113
40:28	104
42:5	118
43:7	12, 99
45:5-7	32
55:8-9	119
65:17	114

Jeramiah

1:5	91
24:8	
46:27-28	5

Ezekiel

18:21, 22	12
28:11-19	37
3:11	12
34:10-13	125

Daniel

2:35	50
10:13	44
10:14	43
10:20	44

Index of Scriptures

Malachi
3:10

Romans
1:25	12
8:14	12
18:19	12

Matthew
1:23	17
1:21	125
2:13	20
2:2	72
11:27	16
11:28-30	106
14:26	125
16:2-3	49, 50
16:18	108, 119
18:10	21
22:30	20
24:35	120
24:37-39	50
26:39	16
26:42	16

28:2-4	20
28:18-20	107
28:19	16

Mark

13:32	16
16:19	112
19:19	

Luke

1:15	15
1:18	20
1:41	15
1:67	15
3:38	87, 96, 122
10:21	16
17:26-27	50
21:25-26	72
23:38	
24:31	112

John

1:1-3	16, 49, 118
1:12	12
1:14	49

1:17	49
1:33	16
1:36	49
3:16	14
4:10-14	30
5:26	29, 122
5:30	16
5:36	109
6:37, 44	16
7:38-39	29, 30
8:31-32	121
9:4	105, 106, 107, 108
10:10	94
10:30	16
11:25-26	84
14:6	16, 121, 122
14:12	110
14:16	15
14:26	15, 16, 109
5:22	16
17:5	16
7:38-39	29
15:26	15, 125, 130, 131
16:13	110, 125, 130

20:19	112
21:15-16	30
21:25	79

Acts
1:8	110
2:1-5	69
2:4	15
9:17	15
17:24-25	29
22:6	33
26:13	33

Romans
1:21-25	127
5:12	112
8:16-17	125

1 Corinthians
15:50	54
15:51	21
15:40-41	53

2 Corinthians
3:6	122

Colossian
1:16	20
1:16-17	43

Hebrews
9:22	88, 89
12:2	108
13:2	20

2 Peter
2:4	20
3:8	38
3:12	113

I John
3:1-2	12, 21

Revelation
4:8	104
4:11	12, 99
7:17	114
10:6	44
11:1-12	29
12:4	37
12:7	20

13:8	108
20:1-3	20
21:1	24, 25, 113, 114
21:23	32, 33, 114
22:5	114

INDEX SUBJECTS

A

Abel 88
Abib 71
Abraham 9, 10, 11, 17, 51, 125, 128, 130
Adam 90, 96, 110, 111, 112, 114, 124, 126, 128
Akhenaten 9
Amenhotep IV 8, 9, 10
Angel 43
Angels 20, 34, 36, 37, 41, 43, 44, 45, 118
Antediluvian 8, 18
Aten 9
Atmosphere 47, 48, 49, 50, 55, 57, 59, 61, 64, 79, 88

Atonement 88, 89
Attributes 7, 12, 13, 14, 17, 20, 97

B

Bara 111, 112
Behemah 87, 88

C

Canaanites 17, 18, 124
Comforter 110, 125
Commandments 4, 38, 101, 103, 104, 118
Creatures 13, 70, 77, 78, 79, 80, 81, 82, 83, 104, 115, 123
Cubits 26, 59

D

Daniel 43, 50

Darkness 31, 32, 33, 34, 35, 39, 40, 41, 42, 45, 114

Day 35, 36, 38, 39, 40, 41, 42, 44, 47, 48, 49, 55, 56, 57, 58, 59, 60, 61, 62, 63, 65, 67, 68, 69, 71, 72, 73, 74, 75, 77, 78, 79, 80, 81, 82, 83, 84, 85, 87, 89, 95, 97, 99, 100, 101, 102, 103, 104, 105, 107, 108, 114, 118, 121, 122, 123, 127, 128

Dinosaurs 81, 124

E

Ecosystem 48, 53, 82, 88, 89, 95, 99

Egypt 2, 3, 4, 8, 9, 10, 11, 12, 32, 34, 70

Egyptian 8, 9, 32, 61, 124

El 10

Elohim 8, 10, 11, 14, 15, 16, 17, 18, 19, 28, 29, 30, 31, 36, 37, 38, 39, 40, 42, 44, 47, 48, 49, 55, 56, 57, 58, 61, 62, 63, 65, 67, 73, 74, 75, 77, 78, 80, 81, 82, 83, 85, 87, 89, 90, 91, 93, 94, 96, 99, 100, 101, 102, 103, 104, 105, 106, 111, 114, 117, 118, 122, 123, 124, 127, 128, 129, 131

Eretes 24

Ergazomai 105

Eternal 29, 30, 32, 39, 51, 83, 84, 92, 99

Exodus 3, 4, 10, 11, 12, 16, 18, 20, 33, 60, 61, 71, 89, 101, 102, 103

F

Fall 8, 12, 89

Father 14, 16, 21, 29, 107, 109, 121, 122, 128

Firmament 47, 48, 58, 60, 77, 81, 123

Index of Scriptures

Flood 2, 12, 18, 24, 25, 26, 27, 49, 50, 109
Flooding 24, 26
Form 23, 28, 53, 57, 62, 65, 78, 83, 84, 99
Formed 27, 28, 32, 33, 34, 47, 57, 61, 62, 90, 91, 96, 99, 130

H
Harvest 68, 69, 72
Heaven 7, 8, 16, 17, 18, 19, 20, 23, 24, 25, 26, 30, 32, 37, 38, 39, 41, 43, 45, 47, 48, 50, 51, 52, 53, 54, 55, 56, 58, 59, 60, 62, 65, 69, 72, 73, 77, 87, 99, 100, 101, 103, 104, 105, 107, 110, 111, 112, 113, 114, 117
Holy Spirit 15, 28, 29, 31, 36, 39, 49, 55, 57, 69, 77, 107, 110, 112, 118, 119, 121, 122, 128, 130, 131
Hovering 28, 42, 57, 77

I
Infinitesimal 1, 5
Isaiah 20, 24, 32, 36, 99, 104, 113, 114, 118, 119, 125, 130
Israelites 2, 3, 4, 10, 18, 19, 61, 66, 88, 124

J
Jehovah 10, 11, 16
Jeremiah 5, 91
Jerusalem 32, 110
Job 20, 37, 43, 45, 91
John 2, 12, 14, 15, 16, 21, 29, 30, 45, 49, 60, 79, 82, 84, 94, 99, 105, 106, 107, 108, 109, 112, 114, 118, 121, 122, 125, 128, 130, 131
John H. Walton 2, 45, 79, 82
John S. Feinberg 12

L

Land 4, 24, 25, 26, 27, 28, 32, 36, 39, 47, 57, 58, 59, 60, 61, 62, 63, 64, 65, 78, 87, 88, 89, 95, 99, 118, 123, 124, 125

Leprous 3

Lexicon 101

Life 1, 21, 23, 24, 25, 28, 29, 30, 34, 47, 48, 52, 54, 55, 57, 59, 61, 62, 64, 65, 66, 68, 73, 75, 77, 78, 80, 81, 82, 83, 84, 85, 87, 88, 89, 90, 91, 92, 94, 95, 99, 105, 108, 120, 121, 122, 123, 128

Light 9, 31, 32, 33, 34, 35, 36, 39, 40, 41, 42, 45, 47, 53, 61, 62, 63, 64, 65, 67, 73, 74, 80, 83, 106, 107, 118, 122, 123

Lunar 75, 83, 85

M

Manna 60

Matthew 12, 16, 20, 48, 49, 50, 55, 72, 92, 107, 108, 119, 120, 125

Ma'yan 26

Memorials 68, 70

Microbes 62, 65, 79, 80, 84

Microorganisms 57, 78

Monotheism 8, 9, 10, 11

Moral 13, 14, 93, 110

Moses 2, 3, 4, 5, 9, 11, 17, 18, 20, 38, 40, 47, 57, 65, 66, 70, 74, 78, 87, 88, 102, 117, 118, 121, 124, 126, 129

Motif 1

N

Noah 8, 17, 18, 24, 50, 59, 60

Non-moral 13, 14, 20, 117, 121

O

Omnipotence 7, 13, 14, 54, 61
Omnipotent 13, 19, 84, 103, 118, 122
Omnipresence 51, 54
Omniscience 7, 13, 54, 61, 79, 89
Omniscient 19, 67, 103, 109, 118, 122

P

Passover 69, 70, 71
Patriarchs 3, 11, 19, 66
Paul 11, 33, 53, 54, 55, 122, 127, 131
Pentecost 69, 72, 128
Peter 20, 38, 113
Plants 62, 65, 82, 89, 90
Prescience 1, 89, 108, 110, 114
Progressive 8, 117, 121, 127, 129

R

Rachel 92
Reconciled 112
Reconciliation 113
Regenerated 112

S

Sabbath 101, 102, 103, 104, 106, 107, 109, 110
Saul 33, 34, 63
Sea 61, 80, 81, 95
Seas 57, 61, 62, 63
Seasons 21, 67, 68, 70, 72, 73, 75, 85, 99, 123
Semitic 8, 17
Seraphim 24, 36
Shameh 47
Solomon 51, 52
Son 4, 15, 17, 18, 72, 96, 107, 112, 115, 125
Soul 69, 91, 92, 93, 94, 95, 97, 106, 109, 110
Sovereign 13, 105, 118, 122

Sovereignty 7, 13, 31, 33, 34, 62, 63, 65, 124
Spirit 8, 11, 15, 23, 28, 29, 30, 31, 36, 39, 41, 42, 49, 54, 57, 69, 77, 93, 95, 104, 107, 118, 121, 122, 125, 128, 130, 131
Subjective 40, 45, 119, 120, 124, 128

T

Tanniyn 81
Time 8, 9, 10, 11, 12, 17, 19, 27, 30, 35, 37, 39, 40, 41, 43, 44, 45, 53, 54, 56, 59, 60, 65, 68, 70, 73, 75, 79, 80, 85, 90, 91, 99, 100, 117, 118, 119, 122, 123, 124, 125, 126, 128, 129, 131

Transcendent 19, 44, 118
Trinity 8, 14
Tripartite 92, 97
Triune 29, 95, 107, 118, 121, 129

U

Us 15

V

Vernacular 8
Victor P. Hamilton's 79
Void 23, 28, 30, 57, 58, 59

W

Weeks 68, 69
Writings 2, 3, 4, 119

Y

Yoke 106, 107, 109, 110
Yowm 35

Made in the USA
San Bernardino, CA
03 January 2018